RELUCTANT STAR:
THE MEL GIBSON STORY

Xmas 1992.
With love
xAlison
& Brian

ALSO BY JAMES ORAM

The Flying Doctors
Home and Away: Behind the Scenes
Neighbours: Behind the Scenes
Hogan: the Story of a Son of Oz
(published in the US as G'day America: the Paul Hogan Story)
The People's Pope
The Business of Pop
The Hellraisers (with Jim Fagan)

ABOUT THE AUTHOR

James Oram was a columnist and special writer for the *Sunday Telegraph* in Sydney, spending twenty years covering stories in Australia, the South Pacific and Southeast Asia. His assignments have ranged from wars to royal tours, from army coups to papal visits. He is now writing books full time. This is his ninth book.

Reluctant Star: The Mel Gibson Story

JAMES ORAM

Fontana
An Imprint of HarperCollinsPublishers

Fontana
An Imprint of HarperCollins*Publishers*
77–85 Fulham Palace Road
Hammersmith, London W6 8JB

A Fontana Original 1991
9 8 7 6 5 4 3 2 1

A catalogue record for this book
is available from the British Library

ISBN 0 207 17108 9

Set in Linotron Palatino and Helvetica by
Falcon Typographic Art Ltd, Edinburgh & London

Printed in Great Britain by
Scotprint Ltd, Musselburgh

CONTENTS

Mel Gibson aged 30 (© News Ltd)

1

The Superstar Farmer from Tangambalanga

The Volvo station wagon drove away from the red-brick farmhouse, bumped through the gateway and turned on to a gravel road, dust pluming behind as it gathered speed. On either side were magnificent gum trees, weeping willows, rolling green hills and in the distance mountains capped by the last of the winter snow. But the driver wasn't interested in what tourists travel long distances to see; he had other, more personal, matters on his mind.

Coming to a bitumen road, the Volvo turned left, passed over a bridge and minutes later entered the main street of a village called Tangambalanga. It passed the Shell service station and the post office, screeching to a stop near the Union Hotel. Not giving a damn that the wagon was blocking the street, the driver got out with the aggressive urgency of someone who has been in a minor accident that wasn't their fault, slammed the door shut and leaned back with his arms folded.

It was Mel Gibson. And, boy, was he pissed off.

His blue eyes were blazing. He could have been Mad Max or Martin Riggs of *Lethal Weapon*, except he wasn't carrying a gun and the only cameras belonged to the reptiles of the press, as the nineteenth-century British cynic, William Cobbett, unkindly described the gentlefolk of the fourth estate. The reptiles were not in Tangambalanga for the scenery. They had difficulty in pronouncing the village's name, let alone spelling it, and would much rather have been in a bar telling lies to one another in Melbourne 300 kilometres south.

They were in Tangambalanga, as was Mel Gibson, because of a story that had appeared in British and Australian newspapers, an unlikely tale that alleged Gibson had left his wife for a nineteen-year-old shop assistant. 'The thirty-one-year-old film actor has moved in with blonde beauty Cassie Kirtson, in a seaside home in Santa Monica, California,' the reports said breathlessly.

Glaring at the assembled reptiles, Gibson said in a voice that had a hint of menace, or perhaps stagecraft: 'Absolute rubbish! It is very distressing to my family and myself. I wasn't even in America two weeks ago. I've been here for months and months. Look, you can see me. Here I am. That is the proof.'

Indeed, he was highly visible. He was wearing a red check country shirt and jeans, his long hair bleached blond by the sun. A casual observer may have noted he wasn't as tall in the flesh as he appeared on the screen. His film biography says he is 175cm (5ft 9in), but he looked more like 170cm (5ft 7in). Still, it was obvious he was speaking the truth. He couldn't have been with 'blonde beauty Cassie Kirtson'. He wasn't Superman, able to streak across to Santa Monica at the speed of light, do whatever one does with blonde beauties, then walk back through the door of his farmhouse like he'd just been outside for a couple of minutes to kick the dog.

And he was blocking the main street.

A car approached. 'Get off the road, you mongrel,' the driver shouted, then recognized the person leaning against the Volvo. 'Oh, g'day, Mel.'

Gibson said he wanted a retraction of the story 'otherwise there will be trouble'. He did not indicate in what form the trouble might arrive – a 9mm Parabellum cartridge or a lawyer's letter – but the newspapers took heed and published retractions and apologies soon after.

On that day in Tangambalanga in 1987 the actor was angry for two reasons. One was that he was accused of fooling around, the other that the media had invaded his privacy by coming to the district he calls home.

Gibson may have had his larrikin days when he drank too much, got into fights, abused reporters, found himself arrested for drunken driving, the sort of problems likely to occur when the booze flows like prohibition is to be declared tomorrow, but he remains a conservative, staunch Catholic. His marriage vows are sacred. Fidelity is among his most important articles of faith. 'I believe in fidelity. It isn't a bad thing to believe in, is it?' he has said. He added on another occasion: 'I am attracted to other people.

Mel Gibson at the Los Angeles premiere of Rob Lowe's film *About Last Night*, 1986

But I believe in absolute fidelity. Anything else would be too messy and unfair.'

Not that he hasn't had the opportunities. He doesn't live in a monastery. He lives in places dictated by his trade, in Los Angeles, Bangkok, New York, Manila, London, Sydney – centres not noted for monastic behaviour. And film crews on location are not famous for living quiet lives. As Stephen Spielberg said: 'Location shooting is the Rites of Spring for certain members of the crew, who may even be happily married, and for young cast members who have never been away from home before. Holiday Inns across America are probably hosts to more spring beds and screaming orgasms when a movie company comes to town than at any other time.'

So temptations are always there, always within drooling distance, like cake shops to a dieter. They have been placed in front of Gibson so often – for after all this is the actor who carries the burdensome label of The Sexiest Man Alive – that had he fallen he would probably now be an interesting specimen for medical research. And they have arrived at the most unexpected times, even when he was being the family man. At a Hollywood party Mel was holding William, one of his six children, when a young, blonde actress decided to try her luck. Sitting down beside Gibson, she ignored his wife Robyn, and delivered the kind of empty chatter that among certain Hollywood denizens passes for interesting conversation. She flirted, she pouted, she wriggled. Gibson and his wife exchanged embarrassed glances.

Suddenly he plonked William on the actress's lap. 'Here, hold him for a moment,' he said.

The actress obliged, happy to be of service to The Sexiest Man Alive, until she realized that William had done what babies do best – soiled his nappies. With a small scream, the woman stood up, saw that her expensive designer dress was no longer totally white, and exited rapidly to the bathroom. Gibson enjoyed the moment immensely.

He enjoyed less an interruption to a dinner he was having with ten people, including Jim McElroy, producer of *The Year of Living Dangerously*, in Cannes during the film festival. A French woman walked over to the table, grabbed Gibson and kissed him like he was her lover just returned from a long absence. Or as McElroy put it 'stuck her tongue about six inches down his throat'. There was nothing Gibson could do to stop it.

He waited patiently until she had finished, then went back to eating.

His reputation as The Sexiest Man Alive, a title bestowed on him by the American mass-circulation magazine *People*, has been boosted by unsolicited plugs from admiring actresses. Sigourney Weaver, his co-star in *The Year of Living Dangerously*, commented: 'Mel is the most gorgeous man I've ever seen.'

After making *Bird on a Wire* with Gibson, Goldie Hawn gasped: 'I think I am in love with him.'

When comedienne Phyllis Diller was asked what she would really like to do in life, she said she would like to have breakfast in bed with Mel Gibson. And so on. The comments never stop. The image is reinforced.

Gibson has spoken of the temptations. 'I know I'm a fantasy figure to a lot of people but, for most, that's as far as it goes. I'm romantic but I wouldn't expect every woman to want to tear her clothes off when she meets me. And I wouldn't respond, anyway. That sort of thing only happens if you're nosing around, asking for it.'

At first Gibson refused to accept that the 'Sexiest Man' tag was part of the Hollywood hype much encouraged by studio publicity flacks. To some flacks it was almost as good as winning an Oscar. Then Gibson mellowed. 'Now I think it's hilarious. . . . Hell, I ain't ugly, but I wouldn't call myself an Adonis either. Entirely too much emphasis is placed on physical appearance. But now I can laugh about it. And I know I'm not the sexiest man alive. No way.'

His mother, the late Anne Gibson, agreed. 'I've seen him first thing in the morning, standing in the doorway, yawning and scratching his chest. Handsome? Not at that hour!' she told Susan Duncan of *Australian Women's Weekly*.

Nor does his wife Robyn consider him to be anything more than the bloke she fell in love with and married in 1980. 'I am not a heart-throb to her,' Gibson has said. 'She hasn't got my poster on the wall. She tells me to do the dishes, feed the kids – it's pretty normal stuff.'

Gibson is far more interested in his family than vacuous titles. 'I get more fun out of being a family man than I get from the glitz and glamour of acting. If I ever had to choose between my career and my family, the wife and kids would definitely come out on top. I like being a dad and I'm a good one. It's a job I enjoy because I like having my kids around me all the time. I learned to be a good father from my own dad and the benefits are wonderful. When I come home after making a movie, I have these little people surrounding me. We play, we talk. They're my friends and I enjoy spending time with them. . . . I'm hooked on fatherhood.'

Towards his family he has an old-fashioned, Irish-Catholic attitude that would shock modern feminists out of their overalls. Not that it would worry him. He has not much time for feminists anyway, saying a few years ago when he was younger and perhaps not as wise as today: 'I think that word, feminist, is bull. Feminist – it's a term invented by some woman who got jilted.'

He explained his attitude to his family this way: 'I've always believed a family should be together. Just the same as it shouldn't have to be that a wife goes to work, she should be at home with them, building that home and making sure there's a secure family atmosphere. I'm lucky because I can afford to keep my wife at home. Sometimes when I'm not working, I'll take a turn at home and look after the children so Robyn can go out. But I must be honest, she does the lion's share of the work. That's a fact.'

His father, Hutton Gibson, instilled in his son the importance of a family. 'Procreation,' he once said when discussing Mel, 'that's what it's all about. Procreation and education. They're the prime purposes in life.'

Gibson enthusiastically followed his father's advice. Robyn had their first child, Hannah, in 1981. Then came the twins, Edward and Christian in 1982, William 1984, Louis 1987 and Milo 1989.

Because of his Catholic beliefs, he does not practise birth control. But he got indignant when Barbara Walters, the American ABC television interviewer, raised the subject. 'The notion that someone can ask you on national television about [your own] birth control,' he said angrily to Australian reporter Nikki Barrowclough. 'It's none of their fucking business.'

Gibson seldom goes on movie locations without his family. Other actors are somewhat surprised when in some distant exotic location they see the Gibson clan arrive, laden with the paraphernalia of a young family, sometimes a nanny in tow. He is no longer The Sexiest Man Alive but a harassed father coping with more questions than have answers. 'I don't like being separated from my family for more than three weeks. . . . I think it's educational for them to get a look at different cultures, different ways people live.'

His mother, Anne, upset by stories that Mel was less than a good family man, added: 'He takes the children on location and when he's home he's always changing nappies. He knows what I went through, and what Robyn goes through with the six babies. He's a real good dad.'

Gibson works hard at being a father and hard at being a husband. Time after time he has stressed the influence of Robyn in his life, the woman he has referred to as his Rock of Gibraltar, his anchor. 'It's a constant you shouldn't abuse,' he said, explaining his relationship. 'That's too easy. You should try to maintain it wherever you go because if you let it lapse, even if you leave home for three or six months, things could fall to bits . . .'

Should he feel the desire, Gibson can take his family to a variety of homes. He owns a large, rambling residence in the Sydney beachside suburb of Coogee, once a boarding house that still has His and Her toilets. When he lived there regularly he was often seen wandering along the street or across the road to the beach, a child or two in tow.

'He didn't seem to like shaving,' a neighbour said. 'He always seemed to have a stubble. And he was forever on the roof of his house, hammering away. I don't know what he was hammering, but he was up there a heck of a lot.'

Fortunately, Gibson has the ability to be able to blend anonymously into the background like a chameleon. He can walk along the street unrecognized, as Sydney show business writer, John Hanrahan, found when he strolled with Gibson along Sydney's crowded streets, then talked to him in a nearby park. 'Along the brief walk, perhaps thirty or forty people passed us,' Hanrahan wrote. 'Not one took a second glance. For the entire hour we spent lying in the middle of the park Mel remained completely at ease as dozens of people strolled past just twenty metres away from one of the world's hottest movie stars.'

Gibson has another seaside house in Malibu, which cost $A3 million, $A5 million or $A7 million, depending on who is telling the story.

But he prefers to live in the Australian countryside, not only for himself but for his family. 'Never in a million years would I let my kids grow up in New York or Los Angeles . . . I want my children to have easy, uncomplicated lives.'

And so he came to a place near Tangambalanga in the Kiewa Valley in northern Victoria, not quite halfway between Melbourne and Sydney.

Kiewa is an Aboriginal word meaning sweet water, an apt description, for this is good country. Not the harsh, brutal plains of the Outback, the popular cliché of television and movies, but a gentle place. Except, of course, during the 100-degree summer heat when the gum trees can explode into flames and the dry, brown grass become an inferno, destroying buildings, livestock, fences and sometimes humans. Not to forget the occasional tiger snake or copperhead, both more venomous than even a Hollywood gossip writer. The first Europeans came this way in 1824. But Aborigines were there before, 17,000 years before, living well on kangaroo, possum, duck, fish, mussels and the fat bogong moth still plentiful across the land. The Aborigines lived to a strict code based on tradition and tribal law.

One example of their tribal law is worth retelling, because it could have been an inspiration for Mad Max or Martin Riggs when they found themselves in tight corners, bullets zipping around them. The story is told in a booklet published by Kiewa Valley Historical Society, *A History of the Kiewa Valley*, Esther Temple and David Lloyd. For a tribal offence, an Aboriginal called Merriman was condemned to stand within a two-feet circle, thirty yards from the tribe's best spear-throwers, each armed with a woomera (a spear-throwing device) and three spears. Merriman's sole defence was a short hitting stick, the proceedings observed by an early European settler.

The first three spears were hurled simultaneously, one at Merriman's right breast, one at the left and one at the groin. Showing he should have been in movies, Merriman knocked the left spear off with his hitting stick and at the same time leapt into the air and twisted violently with his body to avoid the right one, and spread his legs to allow the third to pass through them harmlessly.

The next three spears were thrown. Like Chuck Norris on a good day, he evaded them in the same manner as the first three and was still leaping and twisting when the third volley was thrown. He flicked off the left spear as before, allowed the right to pass under his arm and the third under his raised right leg.

Gibson bought the 240-hectare beef property Carinya (which means happy home) for about $A550,000 (about £250,000) in 1985 after his increasingly handsome fees for *Mrs Soffel* and *Mad Max Beyond Thunderdome*. The farmhouse was not the palatial mansion of a star, more the sort of residence one expects to see in working-class mortgage belts, an outside toilet down the back, a vegetable garden. Three years later he spent $A790,000 (£360,000) on extensions and renovations. Later he bought a neighbouring 80-hectare farm and a 440-hectare property not far away. His small Australian cattle empire was now complete.

He made it an international empire in 1989 when he bought the 8,000-hectare Beartooth Ranch in Montana, USA, not far from where Brooke Shields has a property. In the nearby town of Big Timbers there was considerable excitement at the news, reinforced by the belief that the Gibson name could attract tourists with dollars to spend. 'It hasn't changed the town yet, but it will,' said Daryl Price, the bartender at the Grand Hotel. 'You hear someone say Brooke Shields is in town and pretty soon everyone is out having lunch three times a day, trying to bump into her.'

When Gibson went into the cattle business, he cheerfully admitted he was no expert. Heck, here he was, a guy who had spent half his life with tar under his feet, up to his knees in the dirt and dung of a pedigree herd. In fact he originally had no intention of getting into the cattle business in a serious way; he wanted the land only for a place to breathe.

'I didn't know anything about it when I went down there,' he said in 1986, 'which means you get ripped off a few times. But gradually you get this little stockpile of knowledge and it's just like learning any skill. Even after a year of taking a crack at it, I wouldn't be what you call a good beef cattle manager. I've still got a long way to go.'

He was joking, of course, when a few years later he decribed the breeding of cattle on his property. 'We just get a bull. Get a cow. Put them in a room. Soft lights. Flowers. A bottle of champagne. A little music. And you let them go at it. It's the natural thing to do.'

In fact Gibson has taken cattle breeding seriously indeed, building up an impressive business in Australia and the United States. He got serious when Peter Ford, a sixth-generation farmer, looked after the Australian farm when Gibson was away. Ford and Gibson found they made a good team. Ford stayed, joking that he decides what he wants for the farm and then Gibson goes out and makes another film to pay for it.

The Australian side of the enterprise, called Beartooth International, has 650 commercial breeding cows and is in the forefront of embryo transplanting, using American, French and German genetics. He specializes in Salers, Gelbviehs and Angus because he sees them as ideal for cross-breeding. 'If you stick the three together in one animal you've got most of what you want out of cattle – lean meat, growth, small birthweight, desirable black colour, milk and carcass quality and fertility,' Gibson told the rural newspaper, the *Weekly Times*.

He is building a reputation with his stud, but is aware of the dangers in this most complicated branch of farming. 'We know there are pitfalls in stud breeding,' he said. 'You see studs rise and fall if they haven't got a good foundation . . . You glean as much information as you can out of other people in the industry and then you step up to it and jump in.'

The stud quickly returned good dividends. At the January 1991 Denver Stock Show, the biggest in the world, he sold a half-share in a nine-month-old black Salers bull, Beartooth Formula One, for $A60,000 (£27,000). So when he has played his last role, when he walks away from his last movie set, he will be able to return to the Kiewa Valley forever and produce beef. 'Mel is very serious about the breeding of outstanding beef cattle,' said manager and former owner of Beartooth Ranch, George Ellis. 'I believe he plans on doing it as a major means of income. He's not doing it for the entertainment.'

As far as possible he keeps his properties free of chemicals, not easy in a land where the smallest seedling attracts every pest, every aphid, thrip, mite and goddamn bug known to man. His father, Hutton, taught him the value of natural food. Now he takes the advice almost to excess. 'I have this wonderful new drink,' he told a reporter. 'I get a juice extractor and I shove in carrots, celery, raw beetroot, red capsicum, raw garlic and ginger and, I'm not kidding, you drink a couple of pints a day and you have all this energy.'

Working his property, riding across the paddocks on his trail bike checking the cattle, the fences, the water supply, he has found the freedom he has craved since the lunatic days when he was dubbed The Sexiest Man Alive. The property protects his privacy, although photographers have been known to crawl through the grass and scrub trying to get Farmer Gibson in their lenses.

'I don't have a great big wall with barbed wire and dogs protecting me,' he said. 'That's a waste of time. If something bad's going to happen it's going to happen, but I mustn't worry about these things. You get the odd clown in the bushes with a 600mm lens telling everyone where your address is, which is a little disconcerting. . . . I think their boundaries have to be questioned.'

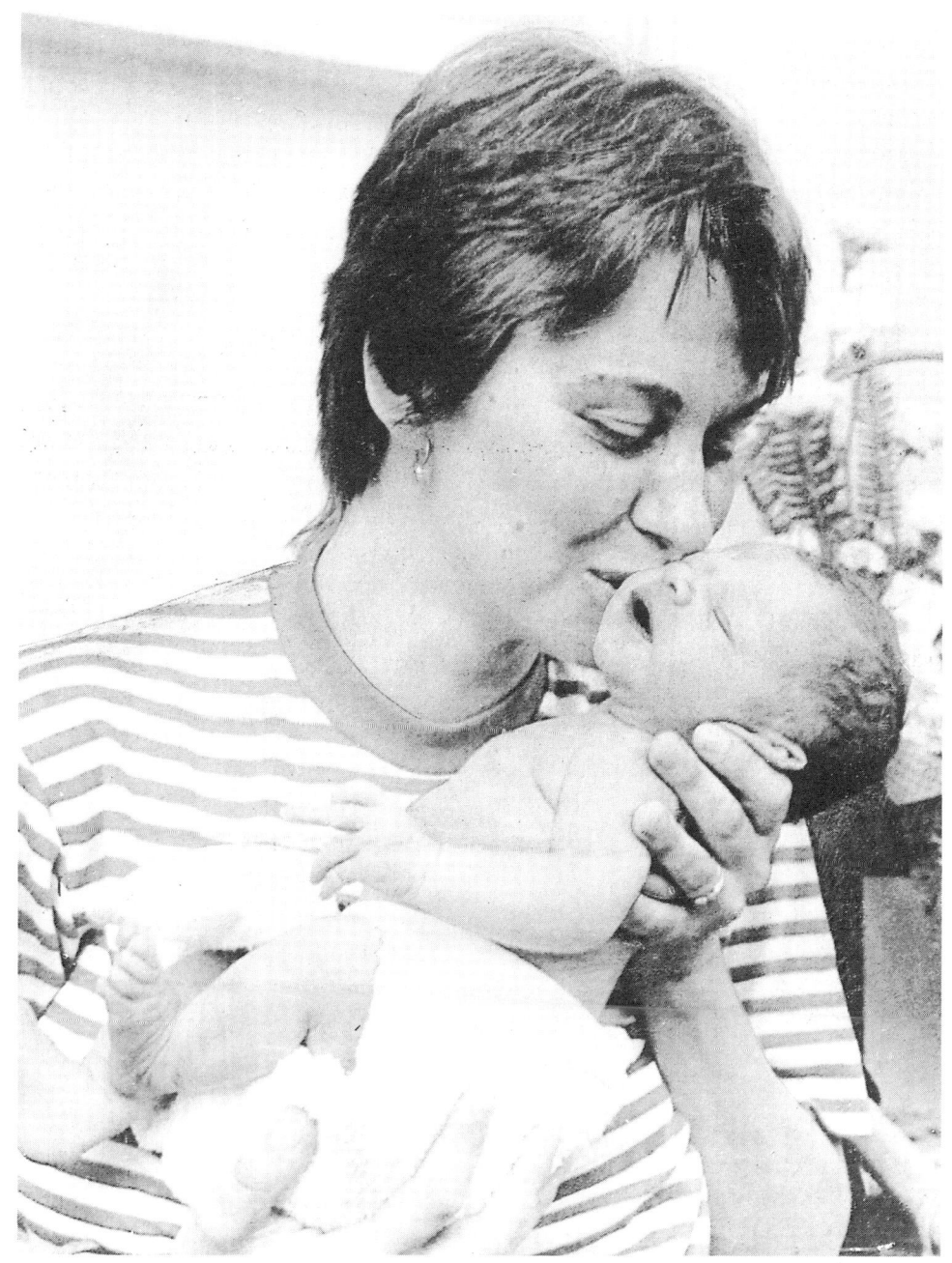

Mel Gibson's wife Robyn with their newly-born first child, Hannah, in 1981

(© News Ltd)

These intrusions annoy him. He agrees with Humphrey Bogart who once said: 'The only thing you owe the public is a good performance.' He takes the family to a restaurant, that's his business. The last thing he wants to cope with is what irked Charles Laughton. 'Every time I walk into a restaurant I get not only soup but an impersonation of Captain Bligh,' Laughton complained.

Mel Gibson is basically a shy person. 'He doesn't like all the publicity that goes with being a big movie star and I can understand that,' Anne Gibson once said. 'He doesn't believe he has done anything to earn all that adulation. Mel is a very low-key person and we don't talk about his movies with him very much when he is at home . . . all he wants to talk about is the fun he is having milking cows and driving tractors.'

Or as Gibson himself said: 'At home I can be myself. I don't have to pretend I'm a movie star. I can watch TV and put my feet up on the table, or go to the local pub and drink beer with guys who don't treat me like I'm something special.'

The Sexiest Man Alive drives regularly into Tangambalanga, sometimes with the kids piled into a Toyota Tarago van, where the 700 or so citizens treat him as anything but sexy. Heads do not turn. Women are not seen to faint in the street. He's just another farmer. They don't want to talk to him about *Lethal Weapon* or even *Hamlet*, but about crops and cattle, sometimes the bloody government, and the weather. Always the weather.

'How you goin', Mel?'

'Not bad. Could do with some rain.'

'Yeah, it's been bloody dry. Dams are gettin' a bit empty.'

'Know what you mean. Doesn't look like rain, either.'

And so on. He might stop at the Union Hotel for a beer, checking the pub notice board for news of the local football team, the Kiewa-Sandy Creek Hawks. He is a local, not a man who can earn $A10 million a movie.

It is of little use asking the pub regulars about Gibson. 'Mel who?' they say, their faces crossed by a look of puzzlement that would win them an Academy Award in Hollywood. 'We don't have any Mels around here. Must have the wrong place.'

Directions to his property are almost as hard to find as a track in the Sahara. 'Mel Gibson? Yeah, I heard he lives somewhere out there. Never seen him myself. Well, they say it's Mel Gibson. Like, I've never spoken to him.' There is a pause while the local scratches his head. 'Mel Gibson, a farmer, here? Bloody unlikely, mate.'

Some appear to be extremely helpful. At first. 'His place? It's down the road about twelve miles, you turn left, take a right . . . hang on, it's a right at the old bridge. Or is it a left? Hold on – Esther! – Oh, it's closed. Been closed for a year now. Well, I'll be blowed.'

They are as protective as only country folk can be. The former publican, Denis Fisher, did say Gibson called in for a drink or two, an ordinary bloke in jeans and t-shirt. 'He has some big name people staying with him at times and always brings them into the pub for a drink,' Fisher said. The reporter's notebook and pen are on alert, ready to record the big names. 'Can't tell you who they are, but I've seen their faces on television from time to time.'

He might call at the post office to collect his mail from postmistress, Betty Faithfull. Mostly his mail has to do with his farming interests, although occasionally there is the bulky shape of a new movie script. Fortunately the post office does not have to handle his fan mail, most of which goes to the studios. If it came to Tangambalanga the post office staff would have to be doubled. After *Lethal Weapon*, Warners got 45,000 letters for Gibson in three months. After *Bird on a Wire* and *Air America*, the studios got a combined 120,000 letters in three months. His Sydney agent, the late Bill Shanahan, who died in May 1991, received about 1,200 letters a month, more than half from overseas.

The Gibson children attend the local school. It is a much, much better place of learning than the first school, which was run by a teacher called Hawthorn, an alcoholic, who got pleasure from belting the bejeezus out of his pupils, sometimes using a fence picket. When he died in a brawl in the nearby settlement of Yackandandah, his pupils gave a mighty cheer and ran to the top of a hill where they lit a bonfire to celebrate.

If he wished, Gibson could attend mass at the small brick Catholic church dedicated to Our Lady, Help of Christians. He chooses not to. This may seem odd for a staunch conservative Catholic who once declared: 'Religion has to be a force in life. Without it, I'd have been dead and buried a long time ago.'

The reason is that Mel Gibson has been having a personal dispute with the Vatican because it got rid of the Tridentine Mass decreed by St Pius V in 1570. The second Vatican Council (1962–65) abandoned Latin and decreed the vernacular could be used in the celebration of the mass, a change many traditionalists saw as a debasement of the image of a timeless and changeless Roman Catholic Church.

Now all this may seem far removed from The Sexiest Man Alive, a movie idol, a farmer who raises beef outside a village the Vatican has never heard of. But it's close to Gibson's heart. He has no time at all for the modern mass, arguing this way to one interviewer: 'In a nutshell, you take an orange which has pips and flesh and peel and all this kind of stuff. You buy this orange from a fruiterer, and you say this is a true fruiterer because this is a true orange. And you go back to the same guy a year later and somehow he has managed miraculously to give you an orange that looks the same, smells the same. But when you open up the skin you find there are only half as many segments. Then you feel you've been ripped off and the whole thing is false. And if the whole thing is false, the practice of perpetrating the fact that you are what you say you are when you're actually not, is a lie. And a grand lie.'

To another interviewer he said he was angry not only because of the changes in liturgy 'but changes in theory. Changes in opinion. A human invention. Opinion. People started leaving the Church when things changed. See what I mean about shifting foundations?'

Gibson's dislike for modernism in the Church is an echo of his father, Hutton, who sees life in black and white and who has never forgiven the Catholic Church for replacing the Tridentine Mass. He believes the new mass is so far removed from the basic teachings of the Church, no valid consecration can take place. Involved with the Catholic splinter group, the Alliance for Catholic Tradition, Hutton has written two books on the subject, *Time Out of Mind* and *Pope Paul's VI's Legacy*.

Hutton Gibson was originally a follower of the French archbishop and thorn in the side of the Vatican, Marcel Lefebvre, who died in April 1991, and was secretary of the Latin Mass Society. But he was sacked after he praised the Anglican Archbishop of Sydney, Marcus Loane, for declining to attend an ecumenical service for Pope Paul VI, writing in the society's newsletter: 'I like bigots. I know where they stand.'

He went on to form the Alliance for Catholic Tradition, with its motto, 'The War is Now.' His detractors call him Pope Hutton.

'The hardest part of my life has been to see my religion fold up,' Hutton has said. 'It has welshed on us, gone away. We can't go to mass, there are no sacraments and I feel cheated.'

Instead of attending church, Hutton gave his children a series of tapes he recorded as the basis of their spiritual life.

And so across the landscape of a small piece of Australia rides Mel Gibson, a movie star, a farmer with dirt on his hands, a family man who makes violent movies, a religious man who won't go to church, a Yank happier Down Under, a paradox on a motorbike, the wind in his face, the sun on his back, the smell of eucalyptus and dung in his nostrils. He feels at home, as though he has always belonged here. And maybe he has.

The reason could be a man called Patrick Mylott who in 1862 decided there had to be a better future than staying around County Mayo, Ireland.

2

Born in the USA

The Catholics always have the best site in town. It's one of the things they're good at, the Catholics, getting a position for their church so that it looks down on all others, particularly the Methodists. So it is in Verplanck in the state of New York. St Patrick's Catholic Church is perched high on a hill above the Hudson River, able to look down on the town and the river traffic. There, in the winter of 1956, Father Daniel Dougherty poured blessed water three times over the head of an eleven-day-old child. 'Mel Columbcille Gerard Gibson,' he intoned, 'I baptize you in the name of the Father, the Son and the Holy Spirit.'

Thus was Mel Gibson named and taken into the Christian faith. But the names. Columbcille, for heaven's sake? What sort of monicker was that for a child of good Irish American stock? Some locals shook their heads, and one quipped: 'He'll be in high school before he knows how to spell his name.'

In fact, Columbcille is a not uncommon name among the Irish. It derives from the sixth-century Irish saint, Columba, an abbot and missionary from a noble family who founded a monastery at Iona in the Inner Hebrides. Gerard came from an eighteenth-century Italian saint who was patron saint of expectant mothers.

And Mel wasn't short for Melvin or Melville. According to Gibson it is the name of another Irish saint, a cousin of the revered St Patrick. There is a cathedral in Ireland called St Mel's.

The names given the young Gibson were proof not only of the family's Catholic beliefs but also the strong links to Ireland, to County Mayo and to Patrick Mylott who in 1862 concluded there had to be greener fields than those of Erin. Except for the ruling British Protestant classes, Ireland was less a land of promise than a place of misery. The Great Famine had killed thousands and political opposition to Britain was becoming violent. Many migrated to the United States. Mylott chose Australia, settling in Tuross on the far south coast of New South Wales, a beautiful place but one of weird, menacing, dangerous creatures – and they were only the insects. Mylott was Mel Gibson's great-grandfather. Tuross, incidentally, is not far, as the crow flies, from Tangambalanga.

In 1871 his daughter, Eva, was born. If there are such things as show business genes, it was Eva who passed them on through the family not only to Mel Gibson but his brothers and sisters as well. His two older sisters, Patricia and Sheila, both sang professionally, another sister, Mary B. studied drama after winning a scholarship at Syracuse University, but eventually decided against acting as a career, and a younger brother, Donal, is an established actor in Australia.

Eva Mylott developed into one of Australia's foremost opera singers, a contralto, who was helped in her career by the legendary Dame Nellie Melba, acclaimed around the world as one of the greatest operatic sopranos of all time. Melba became her confidante and mentor.

Australia being a land of limited opportunities in the opera business – bar songs, yes, arias, no – Eva decided on Europe as the place to study and sing. The Sydney Town Hall was packed for her farewell concert in February, 1902, the windows and doors left open so the hundreds gathered outside could hear her magnificent voice.

After five years in Europe, she went to the United States, giving concerts in Chicago, Boston, Philadelphia and Montreal. Her career was halted when in 1914 she married John Hutton Gibson, a partner in a successful Chicago metal foundry. The couple moved to Mountclair, New York, where Hutton Peter Gibson, father of Mel, was born in 1918. At forty-three, she was considered by doctors to be risking her life by having children, but she insisted. She badly wanted a brother or sister for Hutton. Fifteen months later, after giving birth to Alexander Mylott, complications set in. She knew she was dying, telling her husband: 'It is God's will. We have two wonderful boys. The Gibson name will carry on.'

A month after giving birth to her second child, she died and was buried in Chicago.

The brothers grew up in what was first a prosperous household, but after the Great Depression of the early Thirties reduced the income of the family, they were forced to join other unemployed youths in the Civil Conservation Corps. Hutton was already deeply committed to religion. As he was to say later: 'The greatest benefit anyone can have is to be a Catholic. You have the lifelong satisfaction of being right.'

Entering a seminary, he studied for two years to become a priest but gave it up after doubting he could dedicate his life to the task. In World War II he volunteered for the infantry, graduated to second lieutenant and saw combat in the Pacific until he was wounded at Guadalcanal.

During his army training he met Anna Patricia Reilly, of Brooklyn, but also of Irish background. In fact she was born in Ireland when her mother went to County Longford to visit her own mother.

Anne's sister, now Mrs Kathleen Lyons, of Ozone Park, New York, wasn't too sure of Hutton when she met him. 'I didn't think too much of him, and seeing he seemed likely to marry my sister, there was some defensive mechanism early in the piece. He seemed strong and single-minded, but as we got to know him there was this wonderful warmth, and he truly loved Anne. It didn't take us long to grab her and say, "Don't let this guy get away."'

They married in 1944. Hutton was now working on the New York Central Railroad, the couple living first in Manhattan. Their first child, Patricia, was born in 1955, to be followed by Sheila, Mary B., Kevin and Mauve Louise. Mel was born on 3 January, 1956, in Peekskill, a whistle-stop about sixty kilometres north of New York City, and close by the town of Verplanck, where the Gibson family had moved after outgrowing their Manhattan home.

His birth notice – his first notice of any sort – appeared next day in the *Peekskill Evening Star*: 'GIBSON: Son to Mr and Mrs Hutton Gibson of Verplanck at the Peekskill Hospital, 4.45pm, January 3.'

Hutton, or Red as he was often known because of the colour of his hair, was not a great believer in hospitals, or the medical profession in general for that matter. 'As soon as Anne and the baby could leave hospital, Hutton whisked them back to the sanctuary of their home,' recalled Ed Stinson, a neighbour and close friend.

After Mel, the Gibson family increased. Daniel, Christopher, Donal and

Anne were the additions, with an eleventh child, Andrew, adopted in 1969. 'One more and we could have qualified as a tribe,' Mel joked later.

The family home in Verplanck, on the east bank of the Hudson River, was a modest residence, close by the Sun Oil Company depot, past which huge tanker trucks roared day and night. The house was enlarged frequently as the family grew. Some neighbours recall that the sound of hammering and sawing seemed to be almost permanently heard but even so the house was always crammed, children everywhere.

'One thing you noticed at the Gibson house immediately, there were few toys around,' said Ed Stinson. 'It wasn't just a case of not having the money. The family always seemed to make their own fun and games. They had a special all-in attitude about everything they did for themselves, the family and neighbours. Great friends. Hutton was always a very generous man with anything in life. Some people say he was too generous.

'Most folk remember Mel as a little tyke, dressed much like the kids you saw in those Our Gang shorts at the cinema. Clothes were always hand-me-downs, as were the shoes and boots. But the kids never looked scruffy. Anne and Hutton prided themselves on appearances and manners.'

Because she is Mel's Aunt, Kathleen Lyons can be excused for being prejudiced, her memory coloured by blood ties, but she remembers Mel as 'an adorable child. All the kids were. But he seemed to radiate smiles. If you looked at him, he smiled, you smiled. He could fill a room with smiles. But then he could be very cheeky, and up to tricks a lot of the time. But he was never a bad boy – none of his tricks were dangerous or intended to hurt you. Good-hearted, easy to handle, he was devoted to his mum. As a middle child there was always a lot of protection around him, like an umbrella. His older brothers and sisters really cared for him. Red and Anne ran a tight household, but not severe. The Gibson kids were generally known as being quiet and well behaved and God-fearing. Many families respected them for that alone.'

They might not have had much in the way of spare cash, but the Gibsons ate as well as anyone. Anne Gibson was famed in Verplanck as a cook, her Irish soda bread flan with raisins still remembered with mouth-watering fondness. 'That wasn't her only speciality,' said Ed Stinson. 'She could concoct wonderful meals from bits and pieces. When I worked the midnight shift a few doors from their place, one of the elder Gibson kids

Mother's Day, Sydney 1988. Left to right: Anne Gibson with photo of son Mel; Don Lane, Australian entertainer and TV host; Patricia Hutchene with photo of son Michael, lead singer of INXS (© Greg Porteus, News Ltd)

would always arrive at the oil company office with a midnight meal for me. It was usually a hot meal, and most of the enjoyment initially was guessing what Anne had cooked for me that night.'

Hutton was extremely health conscious long before it became a popular fad. Daily he shovelled vitamin pills into his children, and grew organic vegetables. Even today Mel can still taste the oats his father bought from the local feed store and made into porridge. During the early years neighbours never saw a doctor call at the Gibson house.

At school Mel was considered an average pupil. He could apply himself to any subject he fancied or if it would impress his parents. Even at that early age he had a charm that neighbours and friends still remember. 'A charm or maybe it was devilry,' said Ed Stinson. 'He had great eyes and he'd inherited his dad's strong looks. But despite the average aspects of his schooling, we thought he would be someone important one day. But we never gave the movies a thought. It wouldn't have surprised me to see him try the priesthood or train as a surgeon or lawyer.'

Much of the Gibson family life was involved with St Patrick's Church, a few blocks from their house. Hutton was in the choir, his rich baritone voice still spoken about, and Mel served as an altar boy.

The talents Mel was later to display on the screen began to show at an early age. He liked to act the clown, entertaining anyone around with faked falls from scooters and bicycles, and by walking into walls or doors. 'I think he treated it all as a challenge, to get better and better,' said Ed Stinson. 'Other kids, even members of his own family, would try and emulate his pratfalls. But they were never as good as Mel. Yet, there wasn't any show-off element. Daredevil, yes. Mel just liked doing special feats, and if he made you smile, or laugh, he was happy. There was never any malice in Mel's heart, and I don't think there ever will be.'

Many years later he was asked by Margaret Smith of the Australian publication *Cinema Papers* if part of his personality enjoyed entertaining people. 'Of course it does,' he replied. 'I have been doing that since I was little, standing up and telling jokes. You know how little kids do it. They love the attention – especially if they come from a big family, and I have ten brothers and sisters. I used to get a kick out of affecting people, no matter what sort of effect. That is what drives you on.'

The Gibsons lived in Verplanck until Mel was five. Hutton then bought a small farm, just a few acres, in Mount Vision, about 300 kilometres north of New York City. He still worked on the railroad, staying in New York with relatives during the week, rejoining his family at the weekends. Maybe Mel's liking for cattle came from that period; Hutton bought a few head of beef cattle, about which he cheerfully admitted he knew nothing, hoping they would bring in a few extra dollars for the family. He mightn't have been successful but the cattle did provide entertainment for the children.

Everything was proceeding smoothly, the family was growing up healthily – they mightn't have had much but they had each other – until December 1964, when Hutton's back was badly injured in a railroad accident. Out of work because of the injury, and fighting for compensation, Hutton was forced to sell the little farm, moving to a village called Salisbury Mills, across the Hudson River from their old home in Verplanck.

Looking for ways to keep the family off the breadline, Hutton applied to be a contestant in the television quiz show 'Jeopardy'. He was accepted and won several thousand dollars.

A few years later, in Australia, he again competed on television quiz shows – 'Mastermind', 'Ford Superquiz' and 'Sale of the Century' – winning several more thousand dollars. A reporter asked him if Mel was impressed by his imposing general knowledge. 'He's always known I'm a clever fellow,' said Hutton. 'Actually, I don't think he's terribly impressed – or depressed – about it. His view is the same as mine, that it's got a lot to do with luck. If they ask the right questions, you win. If they're the wrong ones, you lose.'

After another operation on his back, Hutton trained as a computer programmer, while Mel's brother Kevin joined a seminary, and his sister Patricia a convent.

Soon after Hutton was awarded damages for his railroad accident, he got to thinking about Australia, the country his mother had left. He was also worried about the Vietnam War, noting that his eldest son would soon be eligible for the draft. He had no wish to see his sons go off to a far-off killing ground and so, in 1968, he gathered his family around him and set off for a new land.

*　　*　　*

Mel Gibson's school, St Leo's College, Sydney, in 1968 while he was a pupil there

Australia in those days was an uncomplicated place. Although some of the turbulence caused by the Vietnam War was filtering through (heroin was on the streets where before there had been nothing stronger than marijuana, and anti-war activists were busy) it was an easy place in which to live, unsophisticated yet safe and prosperous. The sun shone, the surf rolled cleanly on to the beaches, the streets were relatively safe and serious crime was a feature only in New York newspapers.

Mel Gibson was twelve. His education continued at St Leo's Christian Brothers College, where he wore a uniform with a straw boater which he thought 'weird', and later Asquith High School in Sydney. He quickly learned two things: one was that his American accent could get him into

Mel Gibson (*centre, back row*) in the second form at St Leo's College, Sydney, 1968

trouble with other kids (Americans are still a fairly rare species on the streets of Australia other than those in King's Cross, the Soho of Sydney); the other was that when Australians liked you they tend to insult you, or 'bag' you, as the expression goes. At first Gibson thought everyone hated him because they addressed him in a manner that back in the United States would have started a fight.

He learned fast. At the same time he was a loner. 'I couldn't hack hanging out with a group that did a certain thing. I just couldn't swallow it. I used to think sometimes that these people had something that I didn't. They had an identity.'

He is remembered not for being an outstanding pupil, which he wasn't, but for being a larrikin. And in Australia there is nothing wrong with being a larrikin. Books have been written about larrikins, songs sung, poems composed. The *Macquarie Dictionary* points out that the title was once bestowed on louts and hoodlums, but has been redefined to mean a mischievous young person. At St Leo's he continued the great larrikin tradition by winning a contest among pupils to see who could be strapped most often in one day. According to one former pupil, Gibson was strapped twenty-seven times, his standing among his schoolmates rising considerably. 'I was considered a bit of a larrikin, and a bad influence, but I wasn't. It was just an unfortunate manner I had,' he said.

'I remember him as being a boisterous funmaker,' recalled Ken Coleby, now of Melbourne, a senior prefect at Asquith High School during Mel's days. 'We had to pull him into line several times a week early in the piece. Never for anything heavy or malicious. Mel wasn't like that, he had a controllable energy, was stocky and not easily intimidated. We were continually going to him after mainly crazy stunts he'd pull on unsuspecting people, more than likely the teachers. A couple of the meeker teachers were horrified and thought Mel was too outrageous for his boots.'

Although he appeared in one school play at St Leo's, a melodrama in which he played a villain, he preferred to demonstrate his acting skills away from the stage. With hair down to his shoulders, he walked along the street, normal one moment, the next falling down, pretending to be dead. He fell down stairs to test people's reactions. He pretended to have one arm. He adopted a Scots accent and talked loudly. He staged fights in public places with friends, alarming people around him. The entertainment he derived from this was the reaction on people's faces, especially passengers on trains and buses who would bury their heads in newspapers pretending nothing was out of the ordinary when a young man collapsed with a strangled cry, holding his heart. 'It was a form of escape, I suppose. At that age you've got a lot of pent-up feelings . . . You want to do something definite just to satisfy your mental needs. It's just a con game . . . I used to get a tremendous amount of satisfaction out of that because I was safe. People would treat you in a very different kind of way. . . . My crutch is hiding in someone else's personality. That's an excuse – trying to be someone else – it's a whole different set of rules.'

Not only in the streets would he do his stunts, but also at school. 'He could move very quickly towards a door and seemingly collide with it with a head-splitting sound, a crunch, and fall prostrate to the floor or ground,' said Ken Coleby. 'I mean, he was as good as Peter Sellers doing pratfalls in those days. He was about fifteen or sixteen. Incredibly co-ordinated. Also, he could appear to head-butt his mates, or connect with a wild punch . . . all make-believe, but he had a reputation for being a bit of a devil.'

So much did Gibson enjoy his street games, he was still performing them after he left school. One night he staged a mock fight at the Astra Hotel, near the famous Bondi Beach, with another young actor, Steve Bisley. They jumped over chairs, fell over tables, tumbled down stairs into the street and inspired three other fights. 'We got out of there just as the police paddy-wagon arrived,' said Bisley.

Perhaps his antics were a way of expressing himself. Gibson was not a good talker, at least not in front of a crowd. 'When I was at school I couldn't stand up in front of the class. It was awful. I had the worst fear. I think the reason I was so petrified was because I wanted to and I was afraid that I would be tongue-tied and not able to talk.'

At Asquith High School his American accent was soon accepted. He was called Mad Mel, after an American disc jockey on Sydney radio who, for reasons known only to himself and station management, never appeared in public without a hood over his head. 'They picked on him early,' said Ken Coleby. 'I heard he was roughed up at his previous school, and didn't seem to fight back. Well, that all changed at Asquith. He threw a few real punches and scruffed a few of the boys who had given him a verbal bashing about his voice. Mel showed he could mix it with the best and his schoolwork improved too. I guess he was a rebel in most ways but also did his work at the desk.'

They were good, carefree days. With his Australian mates he went surfing, tried to pick up girls and sometimes succeeded, mixed with a rugby crowd and learned to drink beer. A lot of beer. Drinking beer was perhaps the most important activity for a teenage youth in Sydney in the seventies. Drinking and getting drunk. As he said later: 'There's a terrible macho thing to drinking in Australia. If you don't do it you are somehow considered not manly.'

When he finished high school, just managing to 'limp out', he hadn't anything particular in mind. But his sister, Sheila, did. On behalf of Gibson and without his knowledge she sent an application to the National Institute of Dramatic Art (NIDA) at the University of New South Wales, Sydney, a prestigious institution responsible for some of Australia's best actors. Among his fellow students were Judy Davis, who went on to make *A Passage To India, Golda* and *Impromptu,* and Colin Friels, who starred in the 1990 American production, *Darkman.*

When Sheila told him what she had done, Gibson was not all that thrilled. After considering it for a while he shrugged and said, 'Well, why not? Why not two days out of my life?'

He wasn't confident when he went for his audition, suffering from the shyness he had covered up with such madcap behaviour as pretending to drop dead in the street. But after doing pieces from *King Lear* and *Death of a Salesman,* he passed the audition and was one of twenty students selected that year.

He did not exactly throw himself into his work. On his own admission, he stood back and watched everyone else. It was a year before he appeared in a play, for him an experience so terrifying his legs would not work properly. 'My knees were buckled with nerves. I just rattled off my lines and went off. But you've got to go through that. It's like breaking the sound barrier.'

One of his tutors, Richard Wherrett, remembered Gibson's nervousness at the beginning of a NIDA production. 'Mel was very shy. After the first rehearsal I invited the cast for a drink so we could all get to know one another. We sat in the bar with our beers and he was so nervous he knocked his all over me.'

But he learned. He told Margaret Smith of *Cinema Papers*: 'Actually, NIDA was very valuable. It offers lots of things you have never come across before. You have to go in with the understanding that you try everything, even if you don't like the look of it: "What do we have to fence for? Why do we have to do gymnastics?" – all that sort of thing. Honestly, once you start to get into it, you enjoy it. You begin to appreciate that side of it because it brings out new skills.'

In those days Gibson lived from hand to mouth. He shared a tumbledown house with several other students, described by actor Steve Bisley as a 'demolition site'. He even had to steal to exist. Years later when as an international star he returned to NIDA, Gibson told students: 'We took hamburgers without paying for them on more than one occasion.'

What got him more involved in his studies was a summer job in an orange juice factory. It took him no time at all to realize factory work was not the world's best vocation. He even thought about becoming a journalist. The thought spurred him to work harder at NIDA.

A classmate, Monroe Reimers, now a scriptwriter, said that until the third year at NIDA, Gibson did not really apply himself but was more interested in a good time. 'But in third year he underwent a change, a kind of crazy ambition came over him,' Reimers told *New Idea* magazine. 'He began to play on his image as the leading man. He was always groomed at NIDA for that and it changed him. A part of his personality came out that was quite ambitious, even ruthless.'

Others remembered him as looking more like a surfie than an actor. His classic good looks did not show until his hair was cut for a play. 'Suddenly we all saw this wonderful face. It was as if Mel evolved before our eyes,' said another classmate, Peter Kingston.

What his drama teachers found in him was an ability to move and a talent for comedy, especially the slapstick he had practised as a kid. But it was as Romeo, opposite Judy Davis as Juliet, that caused people around NIDA to sit up and realise he was more than a pretty face. The kid had talent. He might even make some sort of small name for himself. Later he played Romeo for the Nimrod Theatre, Sydney, to warm approval from critics. But back then, in 1975, he was just another young actor hoping the goddesses of muse would notice him.

They did. The result was a movie that in later years Gibson didn't talk about too much. And if he did he was less than kind.

3
From NIDA to 'Summer City'

Phil Avalon heard there was some sort of trouble at the country hall he had hired as production headquarters for the film he was shooting in the area. But he couldn't work out what sort of trouble. He had been forced to vacate the hall for one night for a wedding reception, his cast and crew were enjoying their time off in local pubs, there couldn't be anything that should worry him as movie producer.

Could there? He thought he better check it out because you never knew with a film cast and crew. Looking after a film cast and crew was at times like trying to babysit a volcano. He drove to the hall – and smack into the middle of what could only be described as an angry mob. Not a wedding party happily celebrating the nuptials, not dancing and drinking, hugging and good-lucking, which was what should be happening, but a number of extremely irate people determined to tear Avalon and his car to pieces.

Pounding on the car bonnet and roof, striking the windows so hard they were in danger of shattering, they demanded that Avalon face them. And they were shouting out extraordinary accusations.

'The dirty bastards,' hollered one. 'Who do they think they are?'

'Who? What?'

'Flashin' their bums.'

'Flashing their what?'

'Their bums! Your lot!'

As Avalon said later: 'They were out for blood. They had gone from a happy celebrating group to one that seemed hell-bent on revenge. But I didn't know what they wanted revenge for. All I knew they wanted to bash my head in. I played it as cool as I could because I had to find out what in the hell was happening.'

What he found out was that two of his actors had dropped their trousers, presented their bare backsides to the wedding guests, then disappeared giggling into the night. Such a deed was known as mooning, a sport that had recently become popular in the United States but was not yet common in Australia. One backside belonged to the young Australian actor Steve Bisley, the other to Mel Gibson.

Ten years would pass before the Gibson behind was again exposed to the public view, this time in *Lethal Weapon* when he was seen stepping from his trailer bed and walking to the refrigerator for a beer. The *Lethal Weapon* exposure caused much excitement in cinemas, with over-heated female fans shouting at the screen, 'Turn around! Turn around!' In 1976, outside the country hall, even though the Gibson backside was on display for nothing, the only shouting was for blood.

'My problem,' said Avalon, 'was that I was laughing so much that I had difficulty finding the right words to apologize. I mean, it *was* funny. But not to the family folk at the wedding. While all this was going on Bisley and Gibson were at the local pub quietly wheeling down an ale or two. We got back in the hall the next morning more by luck and guile than approval.'

The movie was *Summer City*, a tale about four friends who go on a wild surfing trip along the beaches north of Sydney. The budget was small, a mere $A150,000 (£68,000) and was filmed in 16mm. 'We were making what was essentially a surfing film to show at clubs and rented halls along the coast,' said Avalon. 'It was something that had been done with documentary-type flicks over the years. Later it was blown up to 35mm for cinema release.'

An actor, screenwriter, sometime model, Phil Avalon raised the budget any way he could, buying and selling second-hand cars, modelling, begging. He didn't even have the full budget by the time he started shooting, only $A20,000 for film stock and processing. Putting out the word he wanted young actors who didn't mind roughing it on location, who were prepared to accept meals that were less than haute cuisine, Avalon was told by actor John Jarratt, already signed for the picture, that Mel Gibson was 'worth having a look at'.

Mel was still at NIDA. It was arranged that Avalon take a look at Gibson while he was rehearsing a play, but what with raising finance, trying to convince investors they were on to the best thing since *Gone With The Wind*, Avalon never had the time. Jarratt, convinced Gibson was right for the role, took him to Avalon's house.

Avalon looked him up and down. 'Yeah, you seem right for the part of Scallop,' he said. 'Not a big part. A support role. But you've got that quietness, shyness, I want. Interested?'

'Uh huh,' nodded Mel, which Avalon took to be acceptance.

'Can't afford to pay you much, though. Only a hundred dollars a week. Four weeks at a hundred dollars.'

'Uh huh.'

'Oh, there's one other thing. We've got to dye your hair blond.'

Gibson hesitated. He mumbled that he wasn't sure it was such a good idea, he was perfectly happy with his hair the way it was.

'Look at it this way,' Avalon argued. 'You'll have a month on one of the best surfing beaches on the coast. You'll be with your mates. And take it from me, there'll be no shortage of girls.'

'Okay,' said Mel. 'I'll give it a go.'

He was taken to a hairdressing salon for the dye job on his hair. When he walked out it was more red than blond. But he was ready for the movies.

The $A400 fee for Gibson was to become something of a controversy twelve years later when Gibson remarked at a Sydney press conference he was still waiting to be paid. He added a few unkind statements about the movie, saying it was terrible and when he realized it was going to be a turkey, tried to keep in the background as much as possible. 'That was why it was hard to see me in it,' he said.

Avalon was upset. He pointed out he still had the cheque-book butts and certified audited financial statements to prove Gibson got the money.

'It wasn't much but the movie was made on a very low budget and I'm sure Mel was pleased to receive the money at the time,' Avalon replied. 'Of course now he is regarded as something like Jesus Christ within the movie industry it must be very hard for him to remember that time. I look back fondly on those days and I'm really disappointed to hear that some people don't.'

Gibson kept up his non-payment claims, like it was bugging him, that is, if he mentioned the movie at all. Often in interviews he skipped over *Summer City*, his memory of making movies starting with *Mad Max*. Avalon, who was building up a reputation as a movie producer, decided matters had gone far enough. 'I feel Mel used to talk about being owed money from *Summer City* as a career colour story,' said Avalon. 'I wrote him a letter – nothing heavy, more of a mate's note – and said the no-pay story was old hat. And I don't think it's been mentioned since.'

Shooting of *Summer City* took place in and around a small coal mining village on the coast, Catherine Hill Bay, about an hour's drive north of Sydney, where the beach produced clean, sweeping surf. The local returned servicemen's hall was rented at $A100 (£45) a week for the five weeks' shoot – except of course for the one night it had been hired previously for the wedding – and it became not only the production office but hotel for cast and crew. Avalon kindly provided mattresses, which were placed on the floor, one room beside the stage reserved for females, the one on the other side for men. The rest of the hall was for wardrobe, make-up, the storage of sets and equipment and interior shots. No one complained. They were all young, including producer Avalon. Sleeping on a floor was no hardship.

Avalon was about to drive to Catherine Hill Bay in his old Chevrolet for the start of production, with Mel Gibson and Steve Bisley as his passengers, when an industrial dispute cut petrol supplies in Sydney. They were stranded. Avalon looked nervously at his dwindling bank balance. He couldn't afford to be away from the location for a minute, let alone a day or two. But luck was on their side, coming in the unlikely form of a car that had crashed over a cliff near Avalon's home at the seaside suburb of Tamarama. After the police and ambulance had gone, and the tow-truck drivers had decided to wait until dawn to haul out the wreckage, Gibson and Bisley exchanged glances and assured Avalon he would have enough petrol.

'Steve and Mel darted down to the wreck with a hose and petrol can and siphoned out enough petrol for us to head off into the night and reach the location,' Avalon said.

For Gibson, *Summer City* was a learning process. He watched, listened and took in everything around him. Avalon noticed his work improving almost daily, over a week the difference was startling. Crew members knew they had someone in front of the cameras who had screen presence, that magical ingredient difficult to define yet as clear as day.

'This guy's got it,' director Chris Fraser said more than once. 'Give him more to do, more to say.'

Avalon noticed also the effect Gibson was having on female members of the crew. The scriptgirl and hairdresser were all but swooning during the screening of rushes (the day's film). Gibson himself studied the rushes closely, sometimes wincing or screwing up his face as he saw his image bigger than life flicker across the screen.

'Hell, is that me?' he would mutter. 'Ooh, the eyes are wandering . . . aah, I'm nodding too much. . . . I didn't know you would be that close.'

Abigail (she answers to no other name), then one of the country's biggest soapie stars, who was contracted for the movie, although not sharing the accommodation in the rented hall, was also struck by Gibson. 'But not so much by his screen presence,' she said, 'but by him as a person. He was quiet, even shy, but he wasn't shallow or transparent. Underneath was something brewing. You could see then the makings of an actor.'

The filming progessed, with Avalon, who also played one of the lead roles, counting the dollars, always worried he was going to run out of money. At the same time word got around the district that the movie was featuring a young man who was worth a second glance, and a third. Girls began turning up on location.

'Mel had plenty of young female admirers from the local community, as well as a lot who were in the area on holiday,' said Avalon. 'He had no trouble attracting girls. But he never really got carried away with it all. He hung around the set when he wasn't on call or not wanted for shots. Some days when he wasn't wanted at all he still spent the day watching his mates do their stuff.'

The film was finished in trying circumstances. Avalon had virtually run out of money, unable to advance even a few dollars for expenses. He had a falling out with the actors but managed to complete the job.

'In the last week of shooting I was absolutely broke,' said Avalon. 'I had to borrow from friends, anywhere I could. We had a local shop catering for us, three meals a day for so much a head. But in the last week I couldn't afford to pay them. I'd go out and buy a lot of mince meat, chop some

'Everything you could want from a leading man – looks, grace and energy.' Mel Gibson in his Sydney hotel enjoying a cigar (© Michael Jones, News Ltd)

onions and carrots into it, cook it myself, and that was lunch. At night they had something similar.'

A couple of years later Gibson reflected on his *Summer City* days. '*Summer City* was a case of wondering day and night if you ate, slept, got paid or what. There was this madness as we went from day to day, a kind of excitement. I don't regret it, though. It was a learning experience. We had to cope with bushfires, slept on the floor of a local hall. It was my first job before the cameras. I would have done anything.'

Summer City eventually opened in Sydney in December 1977, promoted as: 'The one you have been waiting for! Funnier than *American Graffitti.*

Heavier than *Easy Rider*.' It did reasonably well, because it was one of the first movies of its type to be made in Australia, later becoming a cult film when released on video. It even made a small profit.

'I was only twenty-eight at the time,' said Phil Avalon. 'Didn't know much about making movies at all. But *Summer City* sure taught me a lot.' He went on to make bigger movies, including *The Sher Mountain Mystery Killings*, with former world heavyweight boxing contender, Joe Bugner, in a lead role, and in the beginning of 1991, *The Fatal Bond*, with Linda Blair and Donal Gibson, brother of Mel.

Donal Gibson had been in small movie parts before – *Rebel*, *The Punisher*, *Emma's War*, *Blood Oath*, *Resistance* – but *Fatal Bond* was his biggest role. Naturally he was asked to compare his career with that of his brother. 'Mel and I are not the same character and we have different attitudes,' he said. 'If there is any resemblance it has to be in the other person's mind. After all, he's big . . .'

Their mother, Anne, had a different view. 'Mel maintains that he learned everything he knows about acting from Donal, who is a very serious actor,' she said. 'But Donal wants to win success in his own right.'

By the time *Summer City* was released in the cinemas, Mel Gibson had graduated from NIDA. Among those watching the graduation sessions were a number of talent agents, including Faith Martin and Bill Shanahan, partners in a Sydney agency. 'We agents go to the NIDA graduation sessions almost ritualistically to look at the talent coming out of the institute. There have been some fine careers set in motion at NIDA. In Mel's case, he had everything you could want in a new leading man – looks, grace and energy. He was one of the most natural actors I ever saw at such an early stage in his career.'

Not long before his death Shanahan recalled being 'very excited, almost mesmerized' by Gibson's talent at the time of his graduation. Shanahan, later to take over the agency from Faith Martin, still represents Gibson, along with Sam Neill, Judy Davis, Michael Craig, Nicole Kidman, Greta Scaachi and Colin Friels.

In the United States, Gibson has signed with the IMC Agency in Los Angeles, and is personally handled there by Mike Ovitz, one of the most powerful agents in Hollywood.

Soon after graduation Gibson was involved in his second movie. It would make the world sit up and take notice.

4

On the Sets of 'Mad Max'

Mel Gibson knocked on the front door of the Melbourne house. Moments later the door was opened to reveal a man who looked as though he had just left a hospital casualty ward. The man mightn't have been wearing as many bandages as Boris Karloff in *The Mummy*, but was well wrapped up all the same. One leg was encased in plaster, bandages were on his head, shoulder and an arm.

'Ah, sorry,' said Gibson, thinking he was at the wrong house. 'I'm looking for George Miller's place, the film people . . .'

'This is the place,' said the bandaged man.

'I'm Mel Gibson and I'm an actor.'

The bandaged man extended a bandaged hand, grimacing when Gibson shook it. 'Come in, mate. I'm Grant Page and I'm in charge of all the stunts on the film.'

Gibson knew then that second movie was going to be, well, different – perhaps a little dangerous, certainly interesting. The movie was *Mad Max 1*, and already its spectacular stunts were taking their toll. Rosie Bailey, originally cast as Max's wife, broke her leg when her motorbike crashed and had been replaced by a young soapie actress, Joanne Samuel. Filming hadn't even started.

Soon after Sheila Florance, later to play Lizzie Birdsworth in the cult soapie *Prisoner*, broke her knee when she trod in a hole while chasing a rampaging bikie. She was tough, as Gibson later recalled: 'A hell of a dame . . . a few days after being carted off in an ambulance she's back on set on crutches with this gigantic plaster cast and asking, "What do you want me to do now?" If the director had said, "Climb Mount Everest," I'm sure Sheila would have said, "Now, or after breakfast?"'

The Melbourne house Gibson called at in October 1977, just a few days after graduating from NIDA, belonged to the movie's director, George Miller. It was to accommodate cast and some crew. Not quite as spartan as the living quarters provided for the making of *Summer City*, but not the Hilton, either, cast and crew slept six and seven to a room, on camp stretchers, beanbags and mattresses.

During the day, when cast and crew were working, the bikies who had been hired for *Mad Max* used the house to sleep in or do whatever bikies do when they're not on the road frightening people. Before leaving they would scrawl messages on the ceiling to give the actors something to think about before dropping off to sleep.

'Actors are mincemeat – you die today!' shrieked one. Another threatened: 'Watch the roads today – we're out there, you motherfuckers.' Another: 'Care for a lift to eternity, boys and girls.'

As Vince Gill, who played the fatalistic Night Rider in the movie, said: 'It was comforting bedtime reading. Basically, the bikies gave tremendous input into the picture. They were the real stuff, even if they were crazy signwriters.'

Mad Max was decribed as being set in the distant future with urban society 'in terminal decay. The inner city highways have become white line nightmares. The arena for a strange apocalyptic death game between nomad bikers and a handful of young cops in souped up pursuit cars.'

But it was also about heroes, as the character Pete (Fifi) McAfee, the police chief, says to Max: 'They say we haven't got any heroes any more. Well, damn them. You and me, Max, we're gonna give 'em back their heroes.'

It may have been set in the future but it was basically a Western. 'A Western in new clothes,' said director George Miller. 'Each country has its own frame of reference. In Japan they liken it (*Mad Max*) to Samurai pictures. In Scandinavia they say it's a Viking picture. All are basically Westerns.'

The men behind *Mad Max* were George Miller and Byron Kennedy, with the screenplay co-written by journalist James McCausland. Miller, a doctor who graduated from the University of New South Wales medical school, became fascinated with film making. His medical experience was to be called upon not infrequently during the making of *Mad Max* as the stuntmen crashed cars and wiped off motorbikes like it was a long holiday weekend on public roads.

Kennedy, later killed in a helicopter crash, was also besotted with making films. Scraping together the relatively small budget of $A400,000 (£180,000) they set about making a movie that would set new standards in Australian production, as well as influencing any number of overseas producers and directors. Hollywood, always short of an idea but never shy about borrowing one, made several movies with the same theme, all forgettable.

Miller and Kennedy stressed they wanted new faces in *Mad Max*, new talent. At first Miller was keen on signing James Healey, an intense, handsome Irish-born actor, then living in Melbourne. Healey was desperate for a role, anything in fact, that would be an improvement on what he was doing, which was shouldering carcasses into freezers at a Melbourne abattoir.

Healey read the script. He read it again. And what he read he couldn't believe. Next day he saw Miller and told him: 'What are you guys up to? The main character has eighteen lines of dialogue and he's called Max. And the story's about a future gone mad and violent. You've got to be kidding.'

No amount of Miller persuasion could convince Healey to change his mind. Working in an abattoir might not be a picnic, but it had to be better than eighteen lines of dialogue and being called Max. Healey may not have found fame in Australia but went on to a successful Hollywood career – first as Sean Rowan, the scheming, manipulative lover of Joan Collins in *Dynasty*, then as a womanizer and schemer in the soapie *Santa Barbara*.

Meanwhile, back in Sydney, Mel Gibson had got into a brawl. 'It was at a party and three guys really worked me over. I caught the worst of it. A couple of days afterwards I went with a friend of mine to a casting agent who was auditioning for *Mad Max*. I looked a mess. I had cuts, bandages, bruises. But the agent asked to take some pictures of me. I was told that they were looking for rough guys. Soon after that George Miller called me and wanted to see me. When I saw him he offered me the role of Mad Max straight away.'

George Miller tells the story of discovering Gibson this way: 'I was really working on instinct when I cast *Mad Max*. I still remember the moment when I saw the TV monitor with Mel reading this monologue from *Mad Max*. We'd seen hundreds of young actors and I was really tired, but suddenly I thought "God," looked, and I don't know what this is, but there was something special there. I replayed the screen test and the feeling was still there. I forgot I was a director trying to cast his first movie. I sat and watched and got transported by the moment.'

Gibson's pal from NIDA and *Summer City*, Steve Bisley, was also signed, for the part of Max's police force colleague, Jim Goose. The only actor with any profile was Roger Ward but because he was required to shave his head for the role George Miller thought it would not matter. No one would recognize a bald Ward. The first rehearsal and meeting of the cast was in Sydney, and when Gibson walked in, Ward thought, cripes, who's this guy? He doesn't look much.

'I was unimpressed by the rather small, spindly youngster who would play Max,' said Ward. 'But the kid spoke with authority and didn't seem intimidated or frightened to work out various methods and interpretations of certain scenes.'

When the cast moved to Melbourne for shooting, Gibson earned Ward's respect, especially during a scene shot in the ruins of an old gas works. The day had been rough and tough on the actors as they shot bits and pieces of a vital scene. The last filming involved a staircase, and was not an easy task because of the narrowness of the stairs. Cameras and other pieces of equipment were difficult to place. Everyone was getting testy, the cameraman, David Eggby, hot and bothered and George Miller frustrated because of the time it was taking. Time meant money. And one thing the producers of *Mad Max* didn't have was money.

Now it should be pointed out that Roger Ward is a big man. He mightn't be able to play King Kong but could be cast as his younger brother. Let him take up the story: 'Near the end of a long speech I had to walk closer to Gibson, deliver some lines and slap him on the face. Because of my concentration, I was unaware where Mel's feet were and I crunched with my full weight on to his toes. I immediately thought, "Oh, God, there goes the scene." But with amazing self-control – I have since watched for it in the movie – Mel did not even flinch. Nor did I, for that matter. But I was bloody pleased that unlike a lot of other actors Mel did not complain or even mention the incident. It was at that moment that I realized Mel Gibson had what it takes. If I knew at the time how successful he would finally become, I would have stomped on his damn foot a whole lot harder.'

Mad Max was an instant box office hit. Most critics praised it, especially the stunt work. However, Phillip Adams, who was not only a critic but chairman of the Australian Film Commission thought it had all the 'moral uplift of *Mein Kampf*' and could promote violence. But then Adams had always been a supporter of films that few went to see, and was later to observe that Paul Hogan's spectacular hit, *Crocodile Dundee*, was listless and Hogan's performance lacklustre.

Gibson said the violence in *Mad Max* concerned him not one whit. 'I don't see Max as irresponsible . . . I don't think anyone who ever saw a *Mad Max* film went out and mugged an old lady because of it. . . . No, violence in films will only affect those who are sick anyway.'

The film had other critics, too, not ones to influence the public but whose views were important to Gibson, namely his relatives. His aunt, Kathleen Lyons, saw *Mad Max* in New York. 'I was almost out of breath,' she said. 'Sure, I knew it was young Mel up there playing the part, but I'm not into all this screen violence and cars ripping cars apart, and killings. Yet, here was my nephew up there playing the hero and saving the world just like he was as a boy playing and dreaming at home. Even with all that dirt, blood and make-up and the passing of the years, it was little Mel up there, the kid who always wanted to play games and have fun. Now he was being paid to do it, and everything was like a dream. I was very proud of him in *Mad Max* and had to sit in my seat at the cinema for several minutes before staggering to my feet and going outside.'

After *Mad Max* had been screening for a while, Gibson thought he better take a look to see what all the fuss was about, perhaps to check if the audience *was* about to go out and mug old ladies. Quietly entering a cinema, he sat down, only to find it was packed with bikies. 'When it was over, not one of them gave me a second look. Boy, was that a relief. I must admit I didn't like what it seemed to do to the crowd. A lot of them seemed to take it a little too seriously. But I suppose there'll always be those sort of people. I'm just glad a couple of the blokes didn't bother to look at who was sitting next to them.'

A big hit in Australia, Germany and Japan, where it broke attendance records, *Mad Max* did less well in the United States, mainly because its

American distributors demanded it be dubbed. That is, changed from English to English. The dubbing, which was synchronized ineptly, caused a small furore in Australia, where most people considered they spoke English quite well, in fact much better than someone from Brooklyn or the deep south, or Marlon Brando just about anywhere. But a couple of years later the film became a cult hit in America and is still out there somewhere on the art circuit earning money.

Gibson was later to call *Mad Max* 'probably the classiest B-grade trash ever made'. He explained more fully to Margaret Smith for *Cinema Papers*: 'The story is comic-book style and everyone is ready to laugh at it. The images are graphic and cartoonic, so, to slot into that mould, you have to slip into that style. You can't do something totally different; it just doesn't work. Then you have this problem of the character being a closet human being. He has to interact with other characters and yet not appear to. It is a little tricky.'

Even at this early stage, Gibson's charisma, his sex appeal, if you like, was apparent on the screen. Many who paid to see *Mad Max* were young females, who thought Gibson the best thing to come along for ages, or at least since the last rock idol. Roger Ward said that after *Mad Max* had been released for some time, a young female friend of his told him she had seen the film twelve times.

'Well, thank you very much,' said Ward, happy his performance was recognized.

'Yeah,' she said, 'I reckon that Mel Gibson is fabulous.'

Ward said that this was when he realized that no matter how talented an actor may be, his physical presence is what makes him a star. 'I mean, had Mel been an average sort of guy, *Mad Max* would probably have been a workman-like film and Mel would have continued to be a mediocre film actor. But because of the box office success of the film, mostly through the attendance of young female fans, Mel has been rocketed to superstardom. Yet his friend and co-star in the film, Steve Bisley, who has an equal amount of talent but not the same dashing good looks, has had nowhere near the international success enjoyed by Mel. Why? Because the teenyboppers, the twelve- to eighteen-year-olds who make or break a film, are not affected by the way he looks.'

*   *   *

Mel Gibson had made only two movies – and only one had been released – but his name was already being mentioned approvingly among Australia's small but active group of film makers. Michael Pate heard about him from film production manager Betty Barnard who said everyone who had worked on *Mad Max* was raving about the young actor.

Pate was about to shoot *Tim*, from the book by Colleen McCullough. This was no cheap effort, but a serious attempt to bring to the screen McCullough's sensitive story of a mildly retarded young man's relationship with a lonely spinster in her forties. McCullough was hot, as they say in show business, her then latest book, *The Thorn Birds*, an international bestseller, with the film rights sold for a handsome sum to Warner Bros.

And Pate knew what he was about. An Australian, he had gone to find fame and fortune in Hollywood in 1950, and succeeded, appearing in dozens of movies: in *Hondo*, with John Wayne; in Paul Newman's first movie, *The Silver Chalice*; as Chief Sitting Bull in *The Great Sioux Massacre*; as Flavius in the curious 1953 production of *Julius Caesar* and as the Australian coastwatcher Reg Evans, who rescued John F. Kennedy, the skipper of a shipwrecked torpedo boat, in *PT-109*. He was also in *Houdini, All The Brothers Were Valiant, Court Jester, The Revolt of Mamie Stover, Something of Value* and *Major Dundee*. There wasn't a lot about movies Pate didn't know.

Returning to Australia, he had gone into film production, first as an executive producer on Michael Powell's *The Age of Consent*, then as producer of *The Mango Tree*. At first, Pate thought his son Michael, who had just completed *The Mango Tree*, would be ideal for *Tim*. Then he started to hear about a young actor called Mel Gibson.

He checked him out. First he saw a test that had been done by a casting agent. It was promising enough for him to fly to Adelaide where Gibson was working with the State Theatre Company of South Australia. Pate's first reaction was, hell, why have I come so far for so little. A shy, almost inarticulate Gibson failed to impress Pate at the first meeting.

'He seemed to have a closed window attitude,' said Pate. 'And he was having trouble answering my basic questions. Later, after we'd gone to a pub and belted down a few too many, he came out of his shell and there emerged the basic Tim.'

Signed for the role of the spinster was Piper Laurie, with whom a generation of youngsters had fallen in love at Saturday afternoon matinées as they watched her in such costume epics as *Son of Ali Baba*. From the moment she began working with Gibson she was impressed. 'It's incredible when you realize it's only Mel's second feature film,' she said at the time, having obviously not been told about *Summer City*. 'It's not an easy role, yet he brings a warmth and presence you could only expect from an actor who's been around a long time.'

The shooting was done around the northern peninsula of Sydney, an area of outstanding beauty which the cameras captured in fine detail. They captured Gibson quite nicely as well. He was nervous at first, which was to be expected, surrounded by people who had been involved in the making of more movies than Gibson had ever seen. Piper Laurie noticed he made a few mistakes but after three or four days of the six-week shoot he earned respect with his talent, his ability to do exactly what the director wanted and to do it without fuss. He was soon dubbed One-Take Mel.

The character of a retarded person was not easy to play. Movies about retarded persons have not had fans queuing outside theatres, so Gibson moulded the character into what he thought would appeal. 'It wasn't so much playing someone retarded but rather stressing the innocent aspect of it – as if he were someone normal who had a link missing somewhere. I couldn't play him drooling. It would have been a turn-off.'

He said in another interview: 'I'd read the book and I knew how I was going to attack it. It had to be pretty low-key. You can't have a spastic-looking guy. It was more like child-like innocence and obedience. And it wasn't all that difficult   I'm quite simple myself really.'

As the filming progressed Michael Pate looked on approvingly. '*Tim* will be a beautiful picture,' he said to anyone who cared to listen. 'The budget is only $A650,000 but it will look like we spent four or five million dollars on the film.'

Gibson was thoroughly enjoying himself. Not only was he making a movie with experienced people, had interesting dialogue and no worries about money, he was twenty-two, handsome, popular and Sydney was his playground. It appeared to Betty Barnard, the production manager, that he never slept twice in the same place. 'Either there's something of the nomad in his blood,' she said, 'or he's got friends everywhere, because we'd get a series of telephone numbers to follow his wanderings. But he didn't miss a day or turn up late. He's too much of a pro.'

Mel Gibson and Piper Laurie in *Tim* (© *Michael Pate*)

In spite of all their efforts and a good reception in Australia, *Tim* failed to ignite the American box office. But the critics highlighted Gibson's performance. The *New York Post* thought Gibson's portrayal of *Tim* 'a thing of beauty, in its subtle shading of an adult with a very young mind', adding that his 'command of simplicity' was nothing short of outstanding.

Looking back at the film, Piper Laurie said she could not have cast

Mel Gibson attends a wedding in a scene from *Tim*. In the foreground are actors Alwyn Kurts and Pat Evison, who play Tim's parents, Ron and Em Melville.
(© Michael Pate)

Tim better. 'Mel was Tim. It was like Colleen McCullough had written the story for him. He was nervous, anxious, made some elementary mistakes in the first days of shooting, but once he trusted Michael Pate and didn't feel overwhelmed by the other cast members, it was sheer magic. Call it chemistry. And he was fun to work with. When I went back home after *Tim* finished shooting, I told everyone about this wonderful young actor in Australia. Later, when *Mad Max* hit the screens, everyone said, "Wow! . . ." I said, "See, I told you so."'

Colleen McCullough also heaped praise on Gibson. Living now on Norfolk Island, an old convict settlement 1,600 kilometres from Sydney, she still bristles when the subject of film making is raised. The reason is the way Hollywood took *The Thorn Birds* and clumsily made it into a mini-series that cluttered up the screen like a third-rate soapie. Furthermore, it was not even filmed in Australia, the unique flavour of the bush lost in a Californian landscape. Though she was pleased that Richard Chamberlain played the priest, she has never forgiven Hollywood.

But *Tim*, now that was different. 'Mel was absolutely right for Tim,' she said. 'Of course Michael Pate is a shrewd judge of talent. He saw *Tim* as a film, others said it wouldn't translate. It was such a relief to see justice done to a book I'd written. I suffered so much when they did *The Thorn Birds*. If it had gone ahead originally as a movie with Robert Redford in the lead, great. But look at it, a mini-series with Richard Chamberlain . . . oh, it was all too much. They ruined a big story, but that's Hollywood, I suppose. They give you a cheque and tell you to disappear. Yet *Tim*, on a modest budget, worked wonderfully. And I must admit Mel Gibson was one of the prime reasons. He was Tim as I wrote him, as Michael found him and as the audience saw him.'

Members of the Australian Film Institute also saw him as Tim. In 1979 he won the Institute's Best Actor Award for *Tim*, unique recognition for an actor who had made only three movies.

His next movie, *Attack Force Z*, was a disaster. Not that it was the cast's fault. In fact it had the sort of cast that, if used today, wouldn't leave change out of $A10 million. Besides Gibson, there was John Philip Law, who had made a name for himself in *Barbarella*, the New Zealand-born actor, Sam Neill, who went on to star in *Reilly – Ace of Spies* and *The Hunt for Red October*, and the talented Australian actors, Chris Haywood and John Waters.

The story was a typical World War II adventure, in which a bunch of Australian soldiers land on a Japanese-held island and, aided by loyal Chinese, bring back a defecting Japanese scientist. Made in Taiwan, it was a cheap production: the Japanese army never appearing to number more than twenty and shot down so easily they could have been ducks in a carnival shooting gallery. It left audiences wondering how such incompetent warriors managed to capture half of Asia and a considerable part of the Pacific.

After reading the script, Gibson was looking forward to the venture, especially since it would be directed by Phil Noyce, who had won international acclaim for his newsreel nostalgia drama, *Newsfront*. Furthermore, it would be filmed in a foreign clime which sounded a lot of fun. But no sooner had Gibson arrived at his hotel in Taiwan than the dirt hit the fan.

Noyce was at loggerheads with the producers over what he described as 'a new and silly logic' about how the film should look. The problems lay in the fact it was a co-production between a long-established and successful Australian company, John McCallum Productions, which had made the 'Skippy' television series, and Central Motion Pictures Corporation of Taiwan, an outfit best known for films in local dialect, and now making its first English language co-production.

It was the old problem of East is East and West is West and ne'er the twain shall meet. Both sides wanted their best elements given preferential treatment, with Taiwan demanding a Kung Fu sequence to exploit the big Asian following of its stars, Sylvia Chang and Lops Sudsy Ting.

Supporting Noyce, Gibson had several arguments about the way his character, a crack commando, was made to look a fool better suited for cleaning out latrines.

After a few days Noyce, who later directed *Blind Fury*, with Rutger Hauer, *Dead Calm*, with Sam Neill and Nicole Kidman, and *Conundrum*, with Sally Field, was replaced by Tim Burstall, an experienced Australian director. Gibson made it no secret that he disliked working with Burstall.

Lee Robinson, a veteran Australian producer, said Gibson didn't understand the complex nature of the co-production. 'He knew there would be teething problems. But he had this idea the film should be made a certain way. Well, the conditions dictated we should make it another way. And we did. I have no quarrel with Mel's energy and views, but as he was still learning his craft, he should have listened just a little bit more. As for his performance, I thought it was excellent. I am not surprised he rose to the heights of Hollywood stardom. Even on *Attack Force Z* he worked hard, gave it all he had. It shows in the performance. He walked away with his scenes.'

After a while Gibson was pining for the firm control Michael Pate had shown on *Tim*. He was even looking back with fondness to the camaraderie and often undisciplined energies of *Summer City*. Noting the way the movie was proceeding the actors decided they might as well enjoy themselves, which they did with some lengthy sessions at the bar and a few practical jokes.

Chinese guests sitting in the foyer of their hotel were somewhat astonished to see two Europeans dragging another through the front door. The one being dragged had a bullet hole in his forehead and blood running down his face. They hauled him to the reception counter, asked for his room key, and threw him into the lift as though nothing unusual was occurring, the watching Chinese becoming almost scrutable. The two doing the dragging were Neil and Haywood, the one with a bullet hole in his forehead, created by make-up, was Gibson.

Gibson cheerfully admitted he made *Attack Force Z* for the money. 'It was a terrible film,' he said, 'a vulgar attempt at a war action movie with Aussie Wasps shooting Chinese dressed up as Japanese. You do that kind of film because you're starving to death. But there's a lesson to be gained from doing almost anything.'

It look nearly three years for the film to see the light of day anywhere. It found no cinema distributor in any of the main countries, save Taiwan and a few Asian territories. The film finally found its way to video – and only then because Mel Gibson was a big name.

Back in Australia, Gibson continued with the stage work he began while a student at NIDA. It seemed that every time he walked on in a new production, he was singled out by critics, even though he was scarcely a cinema name. His presence demanded attention. In 1979, under the directorship of John Bell, he played Romeo for Sydney's Nimrod Theatre. The distinguished critic, H.G. Kippax, of the *Sydney Morning Herald*, was moved to comment: 'This must be said for Mr Gibson – when his Romeo does grow up, after banishment, the effect is striking. His carriage sheds gaucherie, his voice deepens, he finds nobility.'

He did an Australian play, *On Our Selection*, then took on the part of Estragon in Samuel Beckett's *Waiting for Godot*, one of theatre's more difficult roles.

No Names, No Pack Drill, an Australian play about an American marine who goes absent without leave during World War II, was his next stage venture. A commercial and critical success, the play was later made into a movie, *Rebel*, with Matt Dillon in the role Gibson played on stage.

A season of three one-act Australian plays, under the title of *Shorts*, followed in 1981. During a scene on opening night, Gibson cut a finger which dripped blood over scenery, other actors and even paying customers. The critic for *The Australian*, Viki Wright, found the sight of Gibson's blood so appealing, she devoted considerable space to it in her review. Adding to her pleasure was the fact the leading lady was called, appropriately, Sandy Gore. She wrote that occasionally Gibson popped the bleeding digit into his mouth 'which made his teeth bright red for at least the next seven cynical sentences. Hardly a prop escaped the bright blood, Miss Gore lived up to her name and one lucky member of the audience will have an intimate momento forever – the ravishing Mr Gibson spattered on her white shoes. But while nearly every swooning lady in the audience would have loved to have band-aided the wound, neither of these excellent actors took any notice. I couldn't help thinking (Gibson) may have to carry and pop one of those blood capsules in future – it adds just that extra touch to this powerful play.'

In his next play, *Death of a Salesman*, at the Nimrod Theatre in 1982, Gibson was Biff opposite the Willie Lomas of Warren Mitchell, the British actor who found fame in the television series, 'Till Death Us Do Part'. It was perhaps Gibson's greatest stage triumph. Taffy Davis, in the *Sydney Sun*, called Gibson's performance 'towering'.

It was also one of the Nimrod Theatre's most successful seasons, due in no small part to Gibson's following among young female fans, most of whom had seen nothing on stage but the annual nativity play in the church hall before they caught *Death of a Salesman*. Now they were queuing to get in. And crowding the stage door after the curtain had come down, hoping for a glimpse of Gibson and, treasure of treasures, his autograph. 'We haven't seen stage door business like this for years,' said a pleased member of the theatre staff.

After making *Tim* and *Attack Force Z*, Gibson was much in demand for media interviews. In some he said but a few words, revealing nothing of himself except that he was hating every minute of the interview. In others he clowned about in the same manner he had as a child.

A magazine writer, Liz Porter, interviewed him in a seedy coffee lounge in seedy King's Cross, Sydney, the haunt of characters with backgrounds better not investigated. They were sitting there chatting about this and that when three types, looking like refugees from a B-grade crime movie, slithered in, then glared at Porter and Gibson. Miming the sound of a gun going off, Mel clutched his heart and with his face screwed in agony, slid silently down his seat and under the table. The three characters were not amused, staring at Porter and Gibson with what they hoped was a menacing look. 'We beat a dignified retreat, to continue the interview in a more salubrious setting,' said Porter.

In between appearing on the stage, decimating the Japanese army and taking the mickey out of Sydney hoons, Gibson fell in love with Robyn Moore, an Adelaide nurse. Perhaps he remembered the advice of his parents, which his mother, Anne, recalled: 'He was talking about marriage and families in a general way and asked us for advice,' said Anne. 'Hutton, who's always been Mel's hero, said he should never marry a dumb woman, and pick someone who can always be your friend for life. I added the reasoning of a mum, telling Mel he should always be kind to his wife.'

The couple had known one another for some time before they were married, meeting when Gibson was working with the South Australian Theatre Company in Adelaide soon after making *Mad Max*. 'Robyn and I were actually sharing a house,' he told *Australian Woman's Day*. 'It was just an arrangement, purely platonic. I had to have a place to live and it was cheap lodging at $15 a week.'

Mel Columbcille Gerard Gibson married Robyn Denise Moore in Sydney in 1980.

5

The Triumph of
Gibson's Gallipoli

Gallipoli was a military disaster, a fiasco, a tragedy. The generals and politicians, who were running World War I like it was a board game, the soldiers merely wooden pieces, decided Turkey should be invaded at the Gallipoli Peninsula in the Dardanelles. The force selected to perform this task included men of the Australian and New Zealand Army Corps (ANZAC) who had been training in Egypt, as well as British, French and Indian troops. The main architect of the plan was Winston Churchill, then First Lord of the Admiralty. The Australian war historian C.E.W Bean blamed him for the disaster, saying it was caused 'through Churchill's excess of imagination and a layman's ignorance of history'.

The troops landed on 25 April 1915. When they withdrew in December, smashed to pieces by the Turks, the Allies had lost 33,000 men, of whom 8,587 were Australian.

Australian journalist and author Murray Sayle asked the question: 'Who were the guilty men?' He answered with a vitriolic attack: 'The folks who brought us Ypres and Passchendaele had designed the disaster in the Dardanelles. British generals, monocles screwed into myopic eyes, brass hats jammed firmly down on heads of oak, had ordered these suicidal attacks against impossible objectives, unable to conceive the possibility that their strategy might be mistaken. What's more, they operated from the comparative comfort of . . . the wardrooms of battleships lying well off-shore, pink gins at the elbow. Behind these homicidal idiots stood an even more sinister figure named Winston S. Churchill, a hare-brained amateur strategist who had dreamed up the whole disastrous operation . . .'

Out of disaster grew legend. Gallipoli became a part of the Australian national spirit; 25 April celebrated ever since as the day Australia became a nation. The horror, the futility, the madness was what director Peter Weir hoped to bring to the screen through the eyes of two young Australians who saw the war as an adventure, but soon found it a nightmare.

The movie is interesting for many reasons. It helped give Weir international recognition, which later earned him directing roles in *Witness*, *Dead Poets' Society* and *Green Card*, all big box office successes. Weir became interested in Gallipoli after he finished *Picnic at Hanging Rock* and was thinking of his next project. What he had in mind was a story set in France dealing with the big battles of 1916–17.

'Someone said to me, why don't you make a film about Gallipoli, that's the obvious one,' Weir said. 'The following year I went to London for the opening of *Picnic* and on the way back I stopped off in Istanbul, hired a car and drove to the battlefield. It was an extraordinary experience. I saw no one in two days of climbing up and down the slopes and wandering through the trenches, finding all sorts of scrap left by the army, buttons and bits of old leather, belts, bones of donkeys and unbroken fruit-salts bottles. I felt somehow I was really touching history, that's what it was, and it totally altered my perception of Gallipoli. I decided then and there to make the movie.'

Gallipoli was also Rupert Murdoch's first venture into film making, with another Australian, the entrepreneur Robert Stigwood, until then best known for introducing the Bee Gees to the world. The pair announced, with much fanfare, the formation of a company called R & R Films. Stigwood boasted of an ambitious programme of ten films: 'We plan to make medium budget films and spend about fifty million dollars on the package of movies.'

Murdoch was interested in Gallipoli not only because of the possibilities of producing an interesting, hopefully lucrative film, but because of his father, the great Australian journalist Keith Murdoch, who on 2 September 1915 landed on the shell-blasted beach, saw what was happening and exposed the mess in which the generals had dumped young Australians. He was savage in his attack. 'General Sir W.P. Braithwaite,' wrote Murdoch, 'is more cordially detested in our forces than Enver Pasha [his Turkish opposite number].'

Arriving in Sydney, Murdoch and Stigwood put out word that they were interested in good scripts. Dozens were sent, including the David Williamson script for *Gallipoli*. Murdoch and Stigwood were excited by what they read. 'Rupert and I were up all night reading,' Stigwood said to Weir on the telephone next morning. 'This is the film we want to make.'

But after *Gallipoli* was released, Murdoch and Stigwood lost interest in the partnership, which was dissolved. But neither lost interest in making movies. Stigwood later produced *Saturday Night Fever*, and after buying newspapers, television stations and magazines around the world, Murdoch took over 20th Century-Fox studios in Los Angeles.

Weir always wanted Gibson for the key role in *Gallipoli*. 'I remember first seeing Mel at a film function about the time I was focusing in on *Gallipoli* and how I wanted to tell the story. Having talked with him, seen him at close range, any other choice would have been token or secondary.'

Gibson held Weir in equally high regard. 'I had seen Weir's films and was impressed because they were so full. Peter works on a higher level than I've come across before. Before we started I think he examined every inch of my face under the cameras.'

Coming from America, Gibson had not grown up with the legends of Gallipoli and the Anzacs. Though he learnt about them at school, the feeling, the sense of history, was not a part of him. When he signed for the movie he threw himself into research, reading books by historian C.E.W. Bean, and diaries and letters written by the soldiers, picking up many lines from the way they spoke. He asked questions. Were the Anzacs brave or naive, were they heroes or fools? After all, it was a war fought half a world away from Australia, and its origins were in the assassination of two members of the distant ruling class in a country few Australians had ever heard about. Or as the Melbourne newspaper *Labour Call* observed: 'It is unthinkable to believe that because an archduke and his missus were slain by a fanatic, the whole of Europe should become a seething battlefield . . .'

Reading the books, diaries and letters, Gibson developed a deep respect for the soldiers, their spirit, the way they answered the call to arms. His character, Frank, was an innocent, a bit of a larrikin, but a lad who knew nothing of the outside world, let alone of the horrors of war. He thought it a bit of a lark. Gibson saw Frank as one of the last knights in shining armour fighting the battle in which men were chess pieces in a fearful game. The other main character, Archie, played by Mark Lee, was a kid from the bush who believed the propaganda about the rightness of fighting the Germans and their allies.

'Frank is a professional athlete on a yellow brick road to his fate,' Peter Weir told *Mode* magazine. 'When I saw Mel, his unpredictable quality, his sense of mystery and exuberance added to the part. He is never quite what he appears. The evening he agreed to play Frank I was so excited I took him right over to David Williamson's (the scriptwriter) at eleven o'clock at night so that David could get him as a person into the final script.'

The locations for *Gallipoli* were almost as difficult as the site of the actual campaign, without, of course, bullets, shrapnel and death. The first location was near the outback settlement of Beltana in the lower Flinders Ranges in South Australia. It was hot, well above the century mark, with dust storms adding to the misery. No first-class international hotel was available for the stars, nothing but a shearing shed with meals supplied from the back of a truck. The production department was in a woolshed. The next location was worse – Lake Torrens, an ancient dry salt plain on the edge of the desert, where it was bitingly cold and crawling with poisonous funnel web spiders capable of killing a human.

It came as some relief to cast and crew when they moved to Port Lincoln, a fishing town with pubs and cold beer on the South Australian coast, where Anzac Cove was recreated. 'We embraced the town – and they embraced us,' said Bill Hunter, winner of the Australian Film Institute's award for Best Supporting Actor for his *Gallipoli* performance.

Not that filming here was any easier. The beach and cliffs that were now Anzac Cove were frequently swept by sandstorms during the day, at night drenched by artificial rain. 'All of these conditions brought us a lot closer together and we all felt as though we were not acting, but re-enacting Gallipoli,' said Gibson.

Bill Hunter remembers the long days, from dawn to dusk, the heat, the flies, the sand in the eyes. 'Conditions were bloody tough,' he said. 'It was a record summer for heat, and the odd sandstorm didn't help. A lot of the Anzac spirit came out there. Like the blokes at Gallipoli, we were better than anyone else – better, quicker and cheaper.

'As for Mel Gibson, he was great. Not only was he fun to be with, you could rely on him, he was the consummate pro, always helping people, an

'I would sit up there, often by myself . . . and look down on it. . . . It was a work of art . . . .' The re-creation of the Gallipoli landing for the Peter Weir film, *Gallipoli*. (© R and R Films)

actor to his bootstraps. You could see he was going to be a big name. In fact, if I could have got odds on him becoming a major star I'd have taken a bet and been a rich man now.'

Two veterans of Gallipoli, on hand to keep an eye on the way the younger generation was interpreting their war, were invited to see the film rushes. Everyone in the screening room was apprehensive. If the veterans decided the scenes were a load of bunkum, the film might have to be re-shot.

'Well, what do you think?' someone asked nervously when the lights went on.

Mel Gibson (Frank Dunne) and Mark Lee (Archy Hamilton) all set to fight at Gallipoli. 'Mateship and loyalty is a big thing in me, and I had a lot of mates on that picture.' (© R and R Films)

The veterans said nothing for a while. Their faces were blank. Everyone was silent, leaning forward, waiting for the verdict.

'Not bad,' said one. 'But I reckon there should be more bushes on the left flank.'

The sigh of relief was audible. If the lack of a few bushes was the only criticism, the cast and crew had little to worry about.

Sometimes, when not required, Gibson climbed to the top of the steep cliff to watch the overall scene. 'I would sit up there, often by myself, sometimes with Mark (Lee) and look down on it. I'd think how fantastic the set designer and his team were. It was a work of art, that main set where we shot the landing and the stuff in the trenches. I had huge goose pimples the day they did the master shot of the landing, those little boats going ashore, the Anzacs into the water, scrambling. . . . I had this feeling about what it would be like to have been there . . . scary, futile . . . but it was to be, I suppose, like the Alamo in America. Gallipoli was our Alamo. I felt a kind of constant emotion on many of the days, and that's when I really felt glad I was in Australia doing a movie about Aussies.'

The *Gallipoli* experience left a deep impression on Gibson. Seven years after making it he spoke of 'those memories of *Gallipoli*. I still remember even some of the tiniest details and smallest events from the location shooting. That sort of thing stays with you. Mateship and loyalty is a big thing with me, and I had a lot of mates on that picture. We were like the Anzacs in many ways, on and off the camera. I'm really proud of that film, and it was a hell of a learning experience for me.'

After Port Lincoln, some of the cast and crew moved to Egypt for scenes showing the soldiers enjoying the sights and smells of Cairo souks and marvelling at the pyramids, before leaving for Gallipoli. Gibson called his wife Robyn, then living in Adelaide and expecting their first child at any moment. In fact he called as the baby was being born. 'You can't talk to her,' he was told, 'she's a little busy now.'

The child, born at home, was named Hannah. 'It would have been great to have had Mel here for the birth but things didn't quite work out that way,' Robyn said.

The British reviews of *Gallipoli* were mixed. The *Sunday Times* said it was 'a curious piece of work. . . . By turn sanguine and tragic, schoolboyish and disillusioned, artless and arty.' The *Sunday Telegraph* thought to a large

Mates Billy (Robert Grubb, *left*), Frank (Mel Gibson), Snowy (David Argue) and Barney (Tim McKenzie) mock the pompous English officers they meet in Cairo on their way to Gallipoli. (© R and R Films)

extent it succeeded, adding that its final shot was an 'image of considerable poetic resonance'.

The American critics homed in on Gibson, with *Variety* saying he was excellent and *Newsweek* calling his role 'the most enjoyable'.

Gallipoli picked up many awards, including nine from the Australian Film Institute. Mel won his second Best Actor Award. The film also did rather well at the box office. Costing a mere $A3.4 million (£1.5 million), peanuts for what was after all an epic, it went on to do such good business in London it beat the latest James Bond movie. In the United States it

Mel Gibson and Peter Weir receive their Australian Film Institute awards for *Gallipoli*. (© News Ltd)

grossed around $A6 million (£2.7 million), until then the best figure for any Australian film.

And so to *Mad Max II*, or *The Road Warrior* as it was called for overseas distribution. A summary of the plot begins: 'In a barren, lawless land urban society has been destroyed by the effects of a war which blazed across the oilfields of the Middle East. Fuel is now the only currency of value, the most precious commodity in the world . . .'

It could have been written after Iraq invaded Kuwait and the Gulf War began. *The Road Warrior*, however, was made in 1981, when fuel was still cheap and the only vision of a Middle East conflict was in the imaginations of movie makers.

No one thought there would be a sequel to *Mad Max I*, least of all the two men behind the original, George Miller and Byron Kennedy, and its star, Mel Gibson. 'We all swore we would never get on to that theme again,' said Gibson.

But along came Warners International with a cheque for over $A4 million and, well, what could a fella do. What a fella could do with $A4 million was make a sequel ten times better than the original which cost $A400,000.

The critics adored *The Road Warrior*, finding no end of hidden meanings. 'What Miller has done here,' waxed *Time* magazine, 'is create a milieu as dense and tangy as Tolkien's Middle Earth or Céline's demimonde. This is Australia as the Down Underworld . . . Miller suggests violence; he does not exploit it. He throws the viewer off balance by mixing the ricochet rhythms of his chase scenes with tableaux of Walpurgisnacht grandeur . . .'

Eh? After consulting their dictionaries most cinema goers were none the wiser, preferring to see *The Road Warrior* as a couple of hours of lively entertainment with a series of spectacular stunts, Gibson playing a Shane-like figure who has gone over the top. They saw it as a kind of cartoon played by actors. Gibson himself admitted it was not full of deep, meaningful questions about the mystery of life. 'We weren't out to make a heavy statement about nuclear holocaust. I mean, it's just bizarre. It's so far beyond reality in every way that you just can't take it seriously. As for the bleak outlook, that's a nightmare speculation of one guy, George Miller. The movie goes the first *Max* one better. It is meatier, the story construction is far superior, and there are more thrills and spills. It's just a more artful cartoon . . .'

In another interview he said Mad Max was 'just a caricature of the tall, dark stranger who loped into town on his horse – a formula they found worked years ago in Westerns. The style demanded caricature; there was nothing there to let me strut my stuff.'

The Road Warrior was made 1,100 kilometres west of Sydney, near Broken Hill, a town famous for the mining of zinc, lead and silver, an astonishing beer consumption and an illegal gambling game called two-up which the authorities pretend does not exist. To this arid region was taken a small army of actors, crew and stuntmen, as well as eighty vehicles, most of which would be wrecked.

The stuntmen were the stars. Vehicles as huge as road tankers were rolled, others crashed into one other, careened off bigger vehicles, exploded. In the final two weeks of shooting five stunt people were injured, including one who had his ankle broken when it was kicked by a camel.

Renting a house in Broken Hill, Gibson brought his wife and family to the location. 'He's a strong family man and did not want to be away from them for such a long period,' said Vernon Wells, who played the leathered and mohawked Wez. 'We all worked to a very tight schedule and didn't have a great deal of time to ourselves. We had a lot of 5 am starts and Mel didn't receive any special treatment during the shoot.'

Oddly, some jealousies emerged during and after *The Road Warrior*, all to do with fame and success, of course. Gibson got around $A120,000 (£55,000) for the movie, more than had ever been paid to an Australian actor for an Australian movie. Some actors claimed Gibson let them down by promising to help them, then doing nothing. 'After *Mad Max II* he promised us parts in that film [*The Year of Living Dangerously*] and a trip to the Philippines,' said one. 'Never heard a word from him. He pretends he's never known us.'

One actor involved with *Mad Max* said: 'I have a policy of not talking about Mel Gibson. Why should I? He never talks about me. And that suits me fine.'

Another said: 'In the beginning he leaned on us, begged us to help him, used us. When he got the chance to do something for his mates, he disappeared.'

Bad-mouthing of colleagues is not unknown in Hollywood, in fact it is considered a recognized sport on the cocktail circuit. Australia is no different. But Vernon Wells, who after *The Road Warrior* went to Los Angeles to appear in *Inner Space* and *Circle Man* and co-star with Arnold Schwarzenegger in *Commando*, said the accusations were ridiculous. 'Mel isn't like that at all. He is a serious, caring fellow when it comes to the acting side of things. Sure, he mucks around and plays pranks and tricks when the cameras aren't turning. But there is no way anyone in his position would promise mates jobs on overseas locations. To me, that sort of shit-talk is sour grapes, and very unprofessional. Mel is above all that. He has the utmost respect of his fellow workers. He's done so much to put Australia and Australians on the map. Anyrate, take it from me, there are a lot of arseholes in the acting business, Australia included – especially if they go around saying Mel Gibson of all people owes them favours.'

When *The Road Warrior* was released Gibson went on the overseas promotion circuit for the first time, something he would grow to hate, then later accept as part of the trumpet blowing needed to herald the approach of a new movie.

One trip was to Japan. They love him in Japan, or rather they love *Mad Max*, for here is a Samurai character with whom they can identify. And of course the Japanese were less interested in *Time* magazine's 'Walpurgisnacht grandeur' than good old-fashioned, knock-em-down, roll-'em-over, gore-splattered violence. The Japanese, law-abiding, slow to anger, respectful of authority, revel in cinema violence. Or as one observer said: 'Blood is the trademark of the Japanese film industry.'

Gibson spent ten days in Japan, giving thirty-eight interviews to thirteen newspapers, two movie magazines, four weeklies, five monthlies, seven television and seven radio programmes. When he walked into his Tokyo press conference, there was silence among the seventy journalists gathered at the flash Imperial Hotel. They looked at him, they looked at one another. Where's Mad Max? Where's the leather and energy and violence?

What they saw was a polite young man, a little on the short side, dressed in neat casual gear, his face suggesting he was as bewildered as those seated in front of him. An interpreter at his side, he waited for the questions.

'Er,' one reporter said after a while, 'have you been to Japan before?'

'Same question every foreigner has been asked since William Adams got here,' whispered one Western reporter to a colleague, referring to the seventeenth-century English merchant and adventurer who settled in Japan and started a trading empire.

Gibson considered the question. 'It's my first trip,' he said politely. 'So far it's been fantastic.'

The seventy journalists absorbed the importance of his reply. Then another asked: 'Will you be doing any crazy driving stunts this week?'

Gibson smiled. 'The most fearsome thing I could do here would be to drive around Tokyo.'

The ice was broken. The questions bubbled forth. And so it came about that the subject of violence was raised.

'There is something in violence that is universal,' said Gibson. 'I enjoy watching it although I am a non-violent person. It is a kind of release. Japan is the only country in the world where the crime rate is going down and the Japanese love Max.'

From then on Gibson could have done anything. He could've recited 'Three Blind Mice' and his audience would have noted every word. Judging by the reception, *The Road Warrior* was going to be an even bigger hit than *Mad Max I*, which was Japan's fourth most popular foreign movie in 1980.

While he was winning hearts in Japan, Gibson was being enthusiastically received in the United States, especially by those critics deemed serious. The highly respected Vincent Canby, of the *New York Times*, singled out Gibson with these words: 'Here is a major league film personality. . . . It has something to do with his looks, which are more clean cut than the character he plays in the Miller film, and also with the kind of cool, infinitely pragmatic manner with which he dealt with his existential situation. . . . I can't define "star quality", but whatever it is, Mr Gibson has it.'

6
A Year of Living Dangerously

For his seventh film, *The Year of Living Dangerously*, Mel Gibson was paid $A250,000, a substantial increase on his fee for *The Road Warrior*. Call it danger money, if you like. The danger was not in having to wear elevator shoes for his love scenes with Sigourney Weaver or risking pneumonia for a swimming pool scene during a particularly chilly Sydney winter, nor even from rabid dogs or vicious monkeys or getting pelted by rocks during a demonstration scene when the extras became too enthusiastic. They were minor compared with what happened in the Philippines when Muslim fundamentalists decided the movie somehow insulted Islam.

The Year of Living Dangerously, from a novel by Australian author C.J. Koch, is set in 1965 in Indonesia during the last days of President Sukarno. The threat of a civil war between Muslims and Communists is the big story that Gibson's character, an Australian journalist called Guy Hamilton, is observing and writing.

The period is not one that Indonesia much likes to talk about. The producers knew they would have to look elsewhere for locations. 'Of course shooting in Indonesia was out of the question,' Gibson said. 'It would have been like making a movie critical of the Kennedys in Boston.'

Manila was chosen to replace Jakarta. But, prompted by the fall of the Shah of Iran and the rise of the Ayatollah Khomeini, Muslim fundamentalism was on the increase around the world, including the Philippines. A few months earlier the Manila Film Festival, less a tribute to movie making than a vehicle for Imelda Marcos's ego, had been disrupted by Muslims. Now they considered a film which could not be made in Indonesia, a Muslim country, was no less an insult to Muslims if made in the Philippines.

On arriving in Manila in March 1982, security was provided for cast and crew. Gibson was assigned a large Filipino who followed him everywhere, a .38-calibre pistol under his shirt.

Everything went along fine. Gibson got used to having a large, gun-toting bodyguard virtually living in his pocket. The movie was looking good. After filming had been under way for a few weeks, the telephone rang in Gibson's suite at the Manila Hotel where, incidentally, General Douglas MacArthur had his headquarters during World War II. 'Are you feeling brave, Mr Gibson?' a voice asked.

'What do you want to know that for?' Gibson replied.

Then came the threats. The caller talked of bombs and deaths, adding the chilling message: 'Get out or we'll kill all of you.'

Others connected with the film received similar calls. Jim McElroy, the producer, got one but the caller delivered his threat at an inappropriate time. McElroy was being interviewed by police when it came through and the caller, using a telephone two blocks away, was arrested. McElroy was not unduly worried, believing the calls to be hoaxes or without serious intent.

But there was concern, especially from MGM which had backed *The Year of Living Dangerously* to the tune of $A6 million. With MGM's influence, the Central Intelligence Agency, the Philippines Intelligence Agency, the palace security guard, the police and the army all became involved in trying to track down the threats.

However, the threats continued. During filming in a Muslim village in the Quiapo district of Manila, a crew member was slipped a note by a man in the crowd. It was yet another threat. Peter Weir, the director, made the decision to pull out of Manila and complete the filming in Sydney.

'Either they (the threatening callers) were really extremists who felt that if we weren't allowed to film in Jakarta there must have been a good reason, or they might just have been cranks,' Gibson said later. 'Who knows? In any case we weren't about to stick around and find out, so two weeks before we were scheduled to wrap, we just packed our bags and took off. We missed the plane, too – unlike the hero I play – and had to spend the night in an incredibly sleazy airport hotel with a noisy casino occupying the top three floors. Ironically, much of the footage we shot

'I think we threw off a few sparks.' Mel Gibson and Sigourney Weaver in *The Year of Living Dangerously* (© McElroy and McElroy)

later in Sydney looked more authentic than the Philippine location. If you weren't there, you'd never know the difference.'

Back in Australia snow had fallen on the Blue Mountains on the outskirts of Sydney but the actors had to pretend they were in a place not far removed from the equator. It was there that Mel Gibson and Sigourney Weaver had to do the swimming pool scene and make screen love in a car. They were shaking, not from passion, but the cold.

And it was the love scenes that caused ripples wherever *The Year*

Mel Gibson talking to Sigourney Weaver on the set of *The Year of Living Dangerously* (© McElroy and McElroy)

of Living Dangerously was screened. Gibson and Weaver, who played Jill Bryant, assistant to the British attaché, were compared to other great on-screen couples such as Clark Gable and Vivien Leigh in *Gone With The Wind*. Critic Pauline Kael, a curmudgeon when it comes to handing out plaudits, said in the *New Yorker*: 'A new-style old-time "dangerous" steaminess builds up as Gibson and Weaver eye each other . . . The movie has "hot stuff" written all over it.'

'Yeah,' said Gibson, 'I think we threw off a few sparks.'

But it wasn't as simple as that. Gibson was nervous about going into a clinch with Weaver while cameras rolled and no end of sticky-beaks watched every move. Screen kissing is not the easiest task in film making. Jumping from cliffs or brawling with six Sumo wrestlers is easier. Kissing for the cameras has caused more nervousness among actors than giving an Academy Award speech. It was no different for Mel Gibson. He went to Weir and confessed he had butterflies.

'He said he felt awkward,' recalled Weir, 'so to help him over his shyness I went to the film library and looked at some of the best screen kisses in history. The winner by far was Cary Grant and Ingrid Bergman's lingering kiss in the Alfred Hitchcock classic *Notorious*.'

Weir showed the scene to Gibson. The result had the critics and audiences agreeing that the couple produced fireworks.

'Those scenes, they were just something I hadn't done before,' explained Gibson. 'Sigourney hadn't done them before either. She'd only done two films and she likes powering in. She's the girl who killed the monster in *Alien* – now she has to be submissive, sexy, you know. I had trouble too – the whole love thing – I was a real kid about it. Finally we relaxed. Relaxation is the key to it . . . I had to wear elevator shoes for our love scenes. And when I finally board the plane she's on, she doesn't so much embrace me as engulf me.'

Gibson was always Peter Weir's choice for the movie. After directing him in *Gallipoli* he could see no one else in the role of Guy Hamilton. The producers, Jim and Hal McElroy, agreed.

Jim McElroy had known Gibson for some time, first attracted by the eyes. 'I saw Mel's eyes at a party in Sydney, before he did *Gallipoli*,' said McElroy. 'There were these amazing eyes reflected in a mirror, so I turned around and saw they belonged to Mel. We painted the town red that night after the party, and both of us suffered for days. He was a real party-goer, could hold his own with anyone when it came to downing an ale or two. So along with Peter Weir we didn't consider anyone else for the role. There was no need to.'

To help him in his portrayal Gibson talked to several foreign cor-respondents who had worked in Indonesia during the rebellion. He concluded they were not only splendid drinkers and amusing company, but also ruthless, fearless people who enjoyed living on the edge. They helped him round off the character of Hamilton.

'Hamilton is a hybrid like me,' said Gibson, 'belonging to two cultures but really belonging to none. He's the sort of fellow who goes in boots and all. He takes chances. He gets off on living dangerously. He is like a person taking a journey – things happen to him. He's involved but he's got that trait that cuts it off, very surface. That's his real weak point, incapable of love, I think, which I can understand. I was like that for years until all of a sudden I snapped out of it – that's what made me get married . . .'

Weir himself lived a little dangerously, at least artistically, when making the movie. He chose a woman to play the part of a man. The role of Billy Kwan, a half-Chinese dwarf cameraman, was vital to the movie's success but Weir found difficulty in getting the right actor. Time was running out, production was about to start, when Weir was told of a stage actress, Linda Hunt, who could perhaps do the job. Weir was unconvinced – it wasn't a woman's role – but after screen tests knew she was the ideal Billy Kwan.

In Manila, when she was made up, her European female features changed to those of an Asian male, waiters at her hotel would say, 'Yes, sir,' which she liked not one bit. 'I thought, what's happening to me that I could be mistaken for a man,' she said.

But Hunt got the recognition she deserved for the role – an Academy Award for Best Supporting Actress.

When *The Year of Living Dangerously* was ready for cinema release, Gibson went on the promotion trail he hated so much. He could not relax when talking to journalists, convinced they were more interested in his private life than his movie, that they might get a glimpse of the real person behind the mask. At his Sydney media conference he smoked jerkily and heavily, jumped up and down, clenched his fists and flinched when the flashlights popped.

His nervousness worried Jim McElroy. Looking back on the promotion tour, McElroy said: 'I haven't seen Mel for a while now but, judging from what I've seen in television interviews, he's managed to get closer to mastering the art of handling the media. That's something he lacked in the days we worked together. Mel is two different people, you see. He's Mel the confident and articulate actor. Then he's Mel, the ordinary guy,

'The movie has hot stuff written all over it.' Mel Gibson and Sigourney Weaver in *The Year of Living Dangerously* (© McElroy and McElroy)

shy, who likes to be with the boys, or on the farm with his family. I think for a while in those hurly-burly days when his career rocketed, Mel couldn't really separate those two worlds. Or his two selves. It showed in his PR appearances, and in the stories where he was quoted on several things that normally he wouldn't discuss.'

COLOUR PLATES

1. A night out at a Hollywood premiere with his wife, Robyn
   © *London Features*

2. Early days of success on the Hollywood circuit
   © *Phil Ramey*

3. A fun night out on the town? Or in training for a stunt-packed action film?
   © *Phil Ramey*

4. Beyond Thunderdome – Gibson on the set of *Mad Max III*
   © *UPP*

5. Lethal to the ladies – a sultry Gibson on the set of *Lethal Weapon*
   © *UPP*

6. Three fellow superstars: Mel with Goldie Hawn and Kurt Russell – co-stars in *Bird on a Wire* and *Tequila Sunrise* respectively
   © *London Features*

7. The end of one of those Hollywood nights – when most superstars just want a quiet cigarette
   © *Phil Ramey*

8. The breathtaking view from one of Mel Gibson's Kiewa Valley properties
   © *David Mason, News Ltd of Australia*

9. Mel addresses the crowd during the open day at his Gundowring farm
   © *ibid*

10. & 11. Mel mixes with the locals and fellow cattlemen
    © *ibid*

12. Glenys at the court of Prince Mel: Glenys Kinnock and her daughter join Gibson at the London premiere of *Hamlet*

13. Screen heart-throbs of two generations: Mel Gibson and Peter O'Toole discuss their attempts, twenty-eight years apart, to play Hamlet

14. Gibson shares the triumph of the *Hamlet* premiere with his wife, Robyn
    © *12, 13, 14 Associated Newspapers*

Similar comments have come from others who have worked with Gibson or watched him closely. They agreed Gibson wasn't sure which path to take in his early days. One led to stardom, the other to second billing. Anthony Hopkins, his co-star in *The Bounty*, said: 'I don't think he likes being a star. . . . He told me he was scared at times and that's good because we're all scared. It helps the adrenalin.'

During the making of *The Year of Living Dangerously* Gibson became a father again. His wife Robyn gave birth to twins, with Gibson at her side during delivery in The Women's Hospital, Sydney. 'It was one of the happiest moments of my life,' he said, 'but I've got to stop making Peter Weir movies. Every time I make a Peter Weir movie we have another child.'

7

Trouble on the 'Bounty'

For his next movie, *The Bounty*, Mel Gibson went on location in Tahiti. Now there is something about Tahiti that brings out a certain madness in those who linger too long on its shores. Perhaps it is the sensuous atmosphere, the lagoons, coral sand beaches, palms, the green-clad mountains, the *wahines*. More likely it is the claustrophobia an island can produce, coupled with the splendid Hinano beer.

British actor Gordon Jackson, who worked on the 1962 film, *Mutiny on the Bounty*, said: 'Tahiti's lovely for a week, but six months, believe me, drives you mad, unless you are going to go native.'

Almost twenty years later, actor Anthony Hopkins, after spending nine weeks in Tahiti for *The Bounty*, said much the same thing: 'Paradise can wear a bit thin after a while. If you're on Moorea for more than two weeks you can go stark raving crazy. There's a feeling of confinement on the island. There's also the heat – terribly enervating. After a while you see the same faces at breakfast and it starts to get to you . . .'

In both movies the cast and crew decided booze was about the best thing to help their claustrophobia, or whatever. During filming of *Mutiny on the Bounty*, Trevor Howard was taken by police on to the set one morning after a night in the cells; Richard Harris had a habit of picking bar fights, few of which he won; the Welsh actor Hugh Griffith, a man of immense appetites many of which could be satisfied only from a bottle, enjoyed himself so much he was kicked out by the Tahitian authorities and Australian actor, Chips Rafferty, after a long session in the bar, would return to his room, stick his head out the door and howl like a dog, prompting every other dog in the area to howl back.

Twenty years later some of the cast and crew of *The Bounty* kept up the tradition, with Mel Gibson getting involved in a bar room brawl. It wasn't his first brawl as he once explained: 'I'm smart enough to get myself into a fight. Always have been. But I'm not smart enough to win the damn thing. I always come out the worse for wear.'

The fight in Tahiti came about when Gibson was drinking with several English members of the crew, mostly young guys who were sinking the local brew with gusto. 'We were all going stir-crazy we'd been filming so many weeks, and I think maybe some of the guys ignored local custom and started chatting up the girls,' said Gibson. 'In any case, there was a fight. And those Tahitians are big – six feet across. I tried to get our guys out of there but suddenly this huge gorilla hit me on the side of the head. When one of them hits you, you stay down. Let's just say there was a serious lack of communication for a while.'

One side of Gibson's face was injured. For a while filming had to be arranged so the marks wouldn't show.

Mel Gibson's *Bounty*, or more properly, Dino De Laurentiis's *Bounty*, was the fifth production of the saga for the cinema. The first, made in 1916, was an Australian silent film. In 1933 *The Wake of the Bounty* was made, featuring a young Errol Flynn. Clark Gable and Charles Laughton got together to make a 1935 version and in 1962 Marlon Brando and Trevor Howard played the two protagonists. As well as the movies and a number of documentaries, there are more than two thousand writings on the subject.

One might ask why. Well, the tale of William Bligh and Fletcher Christian has all the ingredients of a great epic: adventure, danger, bravery, cruelty, scenery, obsession and sex. Lashings of sex. As much sex as Hollywood can handle without going blind.

The year is 1787. Bligh and Christian, good friends, leave England on the *Bounty* for a voyage to Tahiti to collect breadfruit and deliver it to Jamaica as a cheap staple food for slaves. The long voyage is in a small boat that Mel Gibson later colourfully describes as a 'little shitpot floating around on the ocean with so many guys on it you haven't even got room to fart'.

Nor room for much else. The *Bounty*, a former coastal trader purchased

Fletcher Christian (Mel Gibson) and Captain Bligh (Anthony Hopkins) on the *Bounty*. (© Hoyts Distributions)

by the Royal Navy for £1,950, was ninety-three feet long and weighed a little over two hundred tons. The crew of nearly fifty couldn't move without standing on one another's toes.

When the *Bounty* sailed into Tahiti, the crew took one look at the island shimmering in the South Seas heat and concluded they had found paradise. In no time at all they were lazing around the lagoons in the company of the sexually open women of Tahiti. Christian impregnated the daughter of the local king. Only Bligh kept himself aloof from what was occurring, watching with distaste the dissolute behaviour of his men. When the time came to sail, the crew weighed up the attractions of Tahiti against the delights of the *Bounty* and found the scales tilting. Some decided they were never meant to be sailors. Bligh had three deserters lashed, the famous mutiny led by Christian took place and Bligh and a few men who remained loyal were put into an open boat. In one of the great displays of seamanship, Bligh sailed the boat 6,000 kilometres to Timor, north of Australia.

Originally the distinguished director David Lean (*Lawrence of Arabia, Bridge Over the River Kwai, Passage to India, Ryan's Daughter*) was to have made the picture. He had arrived in Tahiti with the vague idea of making a screen biography of the British explorer Captain James Cook, but, looking at the lush sensuous islands, thought the raunchy tale of *The Bounty* would be more fun. He got backing from Warner Bros and the script was prepared by Robert Bolt. Warners withdrew after Lean, who had a reputation for going over the top, wanted to make two pictures. Dino de Laurentiis stepped in with an open cheque book.

The *Bounty* itself was built by a New Zealand company, Whangerei Engineering, from the original plans held in the Maritime Museum at Greenwich. But this wasn't the 'little shitpot' described by Gibson. Costing $A4 million (£1.8 million), the 380-ton vessel was built of steel then planked with wood, its 17.6 kilometres of rope came from the same British rope walk which made the original *Bounty*'s rigging, its 4,047 square metres of sail was of Scottish flax similar to that carried by the original ship. Above decks it was an exact copy of the *Bounty*. Below decks it was more like a modern cruiser with luxury cabins, microwave ovens, automatic pilot, satellite navigation and twin 400 hp engines with a range of five thousand miles.

Christopher Reeve, star of the Superman movies, was the actor Lean wanted for the part of Fletcher Christian. But then Lean himself was replaced by the Australian director, Roger Donaldson, who had a growing reputation with his New Zealand-made films, *Sleeping Dogs* and *Smash Palace*. Dino De Laurentiis was still keen on Reeve who was then on a remote island in the Bahamas tanning his muscles and trying to make up his mind.

'There was only one telephone on the island and I remember this particular morning when I had to row over in a small boat to another island to get to a telephone and say "yes" or "no" to a huge pile of money, and to this great, great role,' Reeve recalled. 'I was up half the night before trying to make up my mind and that was one hell of a long boat trip. I felt that I was committed to one thing and had to say "no".'

Reeve felt uncertain about Donaldson, who had replaced Lean, and was concerned about the way Fletcher Christian might emerge from the picture. 'I must confess to twinges of remorse,' Reeve said later about the role he turned down.

Anthony Hopkins had already been signed for Bligh and now the net was cast wide to find the right actor for the part of Christian. Jeremy Irons, Anthony Andrews, the rock star Sting were considered and for various reasons found wanting. Then the offer was made to Mel Gibson.

At first Gibson was not keen on the picture. 'I thought Christian was made to look too weak,' he said. 'Besides, he was hardly in the picture. And I didn't want to get involved in the remake of a film which had been done a couple of times before.'

But after talking to Roger Donaldson he changed his mind. Soon he had fallen under the spell the tale weaves. He became obsessed with his character, read all he could find about the *Bounty*, had a London psychiatrist assess different aspects of Christian's life, even visited the house in the Lake District in Cumbria where Christian was born.

'I discovered he had left his footprint in the lead guttering on the roof and scratched his initials in the metal,' Gibson said. 'I put my foot inside his imprint and discovered it fitted perfectly . . . When I researched Christian I discovered he was more a bad guy than the good guy previous films had made him out to be. Christian was not worldly wise and he had weaknesses just as Bligh had but he was capable of strength when the situation demanded it. He was only twenty-two, yet able to navigate a boat through uncharted waters.'

Anthony Hopkins also threw himself into the character of Bligh, reading, asking questions, observing, then standing back to view his subject with the soldier's training he had received in the army. 'People speak darkly about Bligh as a great seaman, strong disciplinarian and a family man, all of which I found him to be,' said Hopkins. 'That's how I played him: with compassion. Bligh was simply not approachable. His problem was he just wasn't a good captain. But life at that time in the British navy was a nightmare. Even Napoleon could never understand why the British whipped their soldiers. And in fact, a point in Bligh's favour, it was he who petitioned the Admiralty to abolish the cat o' nine tails.'

Filming did not always go smoothly. In fact filming never goes smoothly. A hurricane wrecked several sets, shooting was often difficult on the heaving decks of the replica *Bounty*, Gibson was knocked down

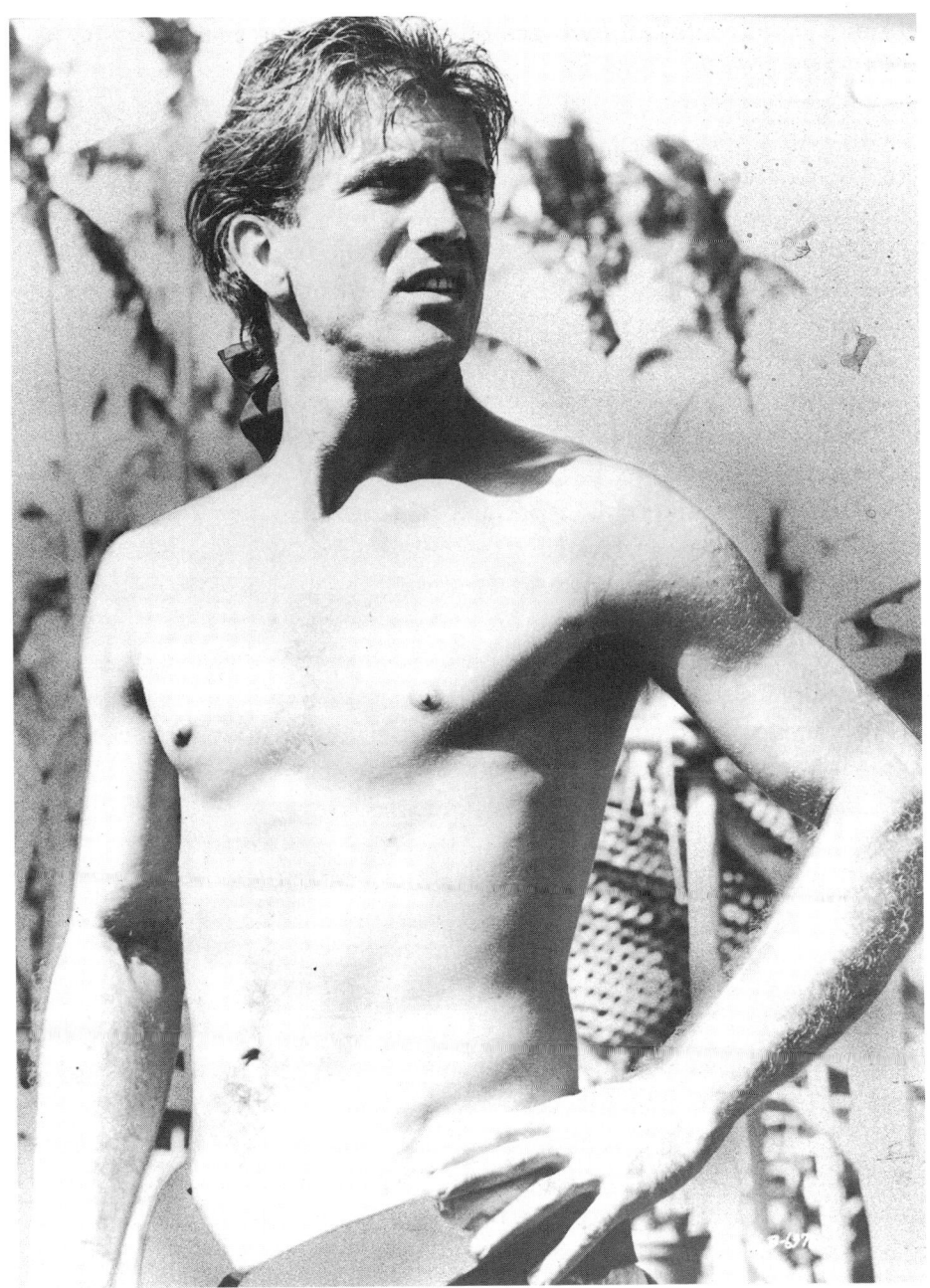

'Old-style' hero Mel Gibson stars as Fletcher Christian in *The Bounty*.
(© Hoyts Distributions)

and washed to the end of the vessel during a storm sequence and director Donaldson was never certain if the action in the can at the day's end would be the same as that in the script at the day's start.

Gibson liked to improvise: not an unusual trait among actors. There is not an actor alive, or for that matter dead, who has not looked at a script and decided it could be improved. And only by the actor, of course. As one unnamed Hollywood screenwriter complained: 'They ruin your stories. They massacre your ideas. They prostitute your art. They trample on your pride. And what do you get for it? A fortune.'

For one of the most important moments in the picture, the scene where Christian tells Bligh he is taking over the ship, Gibson decided he would do a little rewriting of his part. Neither Donaldson nor Hopkins had any idea what Gibson was up to.

'I didn't know either,' Gibson later told Sydney show business writer, John Hanrahan. 'I only wrote the scene that morning . . . The character was lacking and the only place to do something was in the mutiny scene when he flips out. I thought the only way he can do it is by being like a loyal office boy, which is what he was – a loyal public servant. He knew what job he had to do, and got fed up with it one day. The only real threat he could make, as I saw it, was knock himself off and leave them without a navigator. If they knocked Bligh off, then he'd threaten to kill himself – It was in the nature of the Christian character. He went schizophrenic one day. Whacko!'

And whacko Gibson went. Hopkins said later: 'It was totally unpredictable, Mel just exploded and it caught everyone off guard. It was brilliant.'

The Bounty was the most realistic and historically accurate of the movies about Bligh and Christian. No detail was overlooked. A researcher hired from the Victoria and Albert Museum, an expert in the manners and society of the late eighteenth century, checked everything, including the size of ship's biscuits. 'The only thing this film has in common with the earlier ones is the subject matter, but one of the reasons to do this film was to make it historically accurate,' said Roger Donaldson. 'What interested me was the idea of making a film about a group of men in a tight, enclosed environment for a long time and study what happened to them after they get to a place where all their inhibitions can be cast aside.'

Mel Gibson had also done his research with professorial thoroughness. He delighted in telling anyone who would listen that Fletcher Christian had syphilis.

The Bounty cost $US20 million. But in spite of a huge advertising campaign which included, among other gimmicks, love scenes from the picture showing a bare-chested Gibson smouldering among a bevy of bare-breasted girls, *The Bounty* did not perform well at the box office. Some critics were kind. *Variety* called it 'intelligent, first-rate.' Of Gibson's performance, *Variety* said: 'Tailor-made physically to fit the mould of old-style heroes, Mel Gibson gets across Christian's melancholy and torn motivations in excellent fashion.'

But back in Australia the *Sydney Sunday Telegraph* could see no merit in Gibson's performance: 'The only problem with an otherwise fine movie is the casting of Gibson as Fletcher Christian. Despite the work he puts into his performance, his Fletcher Christian is lost at sea. It's not so much that he's outclassed by Hopkins, it's that he's in a different league. When cast in his own mould – as in the two Mad Max films, which are already classics – Gibson is incomparable. But you cannot imagine his Christian even having a drink with Hopkins' priggish Bligh, let alone setting out on a cruise around the world as one of his officers. It's a large weakness in an otherwise admirable film.'

Gibson went from Tahiti to Tennessee for his next picture, *The River*, the story of a farmer who is determined to hold on to his land in spite of increasing debts, falling prices, the ruthlessness of big businesss and a river that floods sometimes twice a year.

The characters, Tom and Mae Garvey, have a lousy time on their farm. These are not idyllic acres for romantic dreaming. It rains. The bank won't come across with a loan. A developer wants to flood the whole valley, including Tom's farm, and build a dam. The rain keeps coming. The cow dies and the tractor breaks down. Crops fail. Prices fall harder than the rain. Mae's arm is caught in the harvesting machine. Tom gets work at a metal foundry only to find he has broken a strike and is therefore a scab. The rain doesn't stop. Tom can't perform in the cot. The rain continues and the river floods. 'I kept wishing that Mel would be sensible, sell up his godforsaken farm and take his family somewhere else,' sighed Australian critic, Evan Williams.

The River was important for Gibson's career because it was the first time he had made a movie in the United States. His previous work was well known in America but his films had all been Australian or, in the case of *The Bounty*, British. Born in America, he was at last portraying an American.

The director, Mark Rydell, who showed a talent for plucking heart-strings in *On Golden Pond*, was at first not keen on Gibson for the role, concerned that the actor had become too Australianized in both accent and manners. But Gibson was determined to play Tom Garvey. When he arrived in England to film scenes for *The Bounty*, he went into training with a dialogue director, then later read the script for Rydell.

'Corn'll be ready to pick in 'bout nahnty days,' he said in a perfect Tennessee accent. Rydell was impressed, as was Sissy Spacek, signed to play opposite Gibson, who is considered to have an ear like a tuning fork when it comes to accents.

In fact Rydell was so impressed with Gibson he was soon telling one and all that the actor was the greatest screen presence he had come across. 'I've directed a lot of great actors, Steve McQueen, Fonda, most of the big ones, but let me tell you, Mel is the most exciting,' he said in the manner of a publicity agent selling a client. 'This guy is a cross between Steve McQueen and Montgomery Clift. If you watch him closely there is an insolence and cheekiness there that very few actors have. Look at those blue eyes and killer smile.'

But Gibson was not taking much notice of the bally-hoo. He remained retiring, almost shy, reluctant to take on the trappings of the big star he was in danger of becoming. For this attitude he was lectured by Hollywood columnist Robert Osbourne. 'There's hope for Gibson but if he is to go the distance he'll need not only to be talented and lucky, but he'll need to be attracted to the idea of stardom,' said Osbourne. 'And frankly, I don't think he is . . . I'm putting my money on Gibson but unless he is willing to play star and push the appeal he obviously has, he too will disappear into oblivion. There is nothing wrong with stardom and without it it is impossible to become box office magic to generation after generation. Let's hope Gibson takes the ball and runs with it.'

Mel Gibson and Sissy Spacek play Tom and Mae Garvey in *The River*.
(© Universal Studios/Terry Bourke)

Gibson was not doing a lot of running. He was playing it slow, his way. The problems, even dangers, associated with stardom had not gone unnoticed by him. He had observed and wondered and questioned. As he told a reporter: 'There is a lot of ego involved, of course, not only in becoming "famous", but in the work itself. I mean, I am my own instrument; not like, say, someone who uses a guitar or flute. We're doing the same thing, except they're doing it with a partner. I've got to use me, and that really makes you look at yourself, centre in on yourself all the time. It's a very fine line, and you can fall off the edge easily. It happens to a lot of people, they just turn into schmucks. I've met a few. Never in a working situation, though. In that I've been real lucky. All the actors, directors, crew and so on, I've got on very well with them all: professionals, you see.'

The location for *The River* was in the Holston Valley in eastern Tennessee. Gibson, his wife Robyn and three children with him, was to see how a big American studio spent money – $US20 million, to be precise – on making a film. In Australia he was used to improvisation, to cutting corners, to saving a few dollars here, a few hours there.

A twenty-six hectare block of land was levelled and planted with corn which was force grown in a few weeks through the use of chemicals. A farmhouse, barn, utility sheds and corn cribs were built, then aged to give them the look of being around a few years. A few miles upstream on the Holston river a dam and levees were built, the dam capable of flooding the farm to a depth of 1.6 metres.

For the flood scenes, Gibson spent hours up to his waist in water and mud. When he had finished, he showed his sense of humour by standing on his head and letting the water pour out of his hipboots.

For another scene he was required to look reasonably smart with a baseball bat, a piece of sporting equipment he had not picked up since leaving America at the age of twelve. He found it no trouble at all. 'He smashed the ball long and hard,' said Rydell. 'We only did three or four takes. Although Mel didn't quite hit one out of the park, he was a hit with quite a few girls who were on the set.'

He thoroughly enjoyed making the movie. His children were frequently on location, sometimes interrupting filming by forgetting the order to remain silent, and he liked the way the farming folk of the valley accepted him and his family. 'The expression of southern hospitality is not a cliché and it's not phoney,' he said. 'They are probably the most hospitable people I've ever come across. If you've ever been down south you'd know what I mean. They're fabulous. They didn't know who we were, they just knew we were new neighbours.'

Gibson was disappointed when *The River* failed to set the box office alight, or even aglow. He thought the movie the best he had done until then but the public, perhaps sated by too many films about farmers in trouble – *Places in the Heart* and *Country* had just been released – did not form queues in front of theatres.

However, *The River* changed Mel Gibson's life. It inspired him to sink some of his own earnings into a country property, preferably one that was flood free.

Roger Ward, who had worked with Gibson on *Mad Max*, recalled talking to him during the making of *Mad Max Beyond Thunderdome*. 'I hadn't seen Mel for about eighteen months or two years, but I met a few of the guys on *Thunderdome* and I remember kidding Mel about wanting to be a cow-cocky (dairy farmer). He told me he wasn't into dairying, but cattle-breeding. He'd been hooked on getting a property as *The River*'s shoot continued. Mel and Robyn had their hearts set on getting a farm, and a big one at that. I think that dream of a farm helped Mel get through the trials and tribulations of *Thunderdome*. He really looked a mess at the end-of-shoot party I went to in Sydney. Next thing I know Mel's a country squire at some place down south . . . the Kiewa Valley, but don't ask me to tell you the name of the town. It's a real mouthful.'

But that was in the future. Gibson had another movie to make. As soon as he had finished *The River*, he went to Canada to star in *Mrs Soffel*. It was to be a memorable experience.

8

Mel Gibson meets Diane Keaton

On an April evening in 1984, Randy Caddell, a twenty-three-year-old mechanic, was driving along Yonge Street, Toronto. There was nothing special about the evening. It was typical for April, the temperature around the level that makes brass monkeys nervous. And Randy was not thinking of anything in particular; certainly it had not crossed his mind that in a few moments he would brush briefly with fame.

Stopping for a red light, he looked at his watch and noted it was 8.30pm. Then fame hit him in the backside. There was a crunch, the sound of shattering glass, his vehicle shuddered. A glance in the mirror showed a car had gone right up his rear.

More than a little annoyed, Randy leapt from his car and, frothing with righteous indignation, ran to the vehicle behind him, a 1984 Pontiac, snatched its keys and hopped about like a bare-footed kid on hot asphalt, spouting words historically associated with sailors.

As he said later: 'I was so mad I was doing a little dance in the street and using some terrible language. I mean, I was dangerous.'

The driver looked perturbed, as well he might. Holding up a hand, he said: 'Hey, I'm for love, not war. How about we have a beer.'

Randy wasn't interested in a beer. Not right then. He was too angry. By now a small crowd had gathered, as small crowds tend to do at road accidents, hoping for a smattering of blood and guts. But there was little damage; a few hundred dollars covered the dents in both cars with enough left over for those beers.

'Hey,' someone in the crowd shouted. 'Don't you know who that is?'

Randy nodded vigorously. 'Yeah, that's the sonovabitch who drove into me.'

'Haven't you seen *The Road Warrior*?' another voice called.

Taking a fresh look at the driver of the Pontiac, Randy blinked. The face was familiar and so were the blue eyes. Sure enough, it was Mad Max himself. 'Oooh heck,' Randy said to himself, 'this is not going to be a great day.'

When the police arrived, Mel Gibson was taken to the Five District traffic station where breath tests showed he was over the legal limit of alcohol allowed for drivers. He had between 0.12 and 0.13 per cent alcohol in his blood. The legal limit in Canada is 0.08.

His arrest illuminated the front pages of newspapers in Australia with much prominence given to the fact he faced charges that carried a $A2,000 fine and six months in jail. Some friends were worried it could ruin his career. His agents were working the telephones.

Also worried was MGM-UA. Hearing of the charges against him, studio executives immediately began thinking about the twenty million or so dollars they had invested in Gibson and the movie, *Mrs Soffel*, he was making in and near Toronto. Six months in the slammer, for pete's sake, they muttered, dreaming up the worst scenario. What the hell was the asshole up to? *Mrs Soffel* might be about convicts but, for chrissakes, Gibson didn't have to be a method actor and join them. The more they thought about it, the more their ulcers burned. They did what good Hollywood executives do in moments of crisis – they got a top troubleshooting lawyer and dispatched him rapidly to Toronto.

While this was going on Randy Caddell had calmed down and thought about the driver of the Pontiac. It wasn't a real bad accident, after all. And he liked the *Mad Max* films. He remembered the invitation to share a drink. Yeah, he would have a beer with old Mad Max.

'I just wanted to tell him I didn't regret taking his car keys, but I did regret all the yelling I did at him,' he said.

At the hotel where Gibson was staying Randy was unable to locate him. He knew he was at the right hotel because in the lobby were a couple of teenagers, one of whom, after hearing he had met Gibson, asked, 'Can we touch you?' But there was no sign of Mad Max.

Randy never got to have a beer with Mel.

On 2 May 1984, Gibson had his day in court. Old City Hall, where he appeared, was more like a film première than a place of justice, with fans outside squealing their approval as he arrived. More fans were inside. One female tried unsuccessfully to pass her telephone number to the star.

When proceedings got under way before Ontario Provincial Court judge, George Carter, Gibson pleaded guilty to the charge. The judge agreed with Gibson's lawyer, William Trudell, that the alcohol levels were 'on the low side'. Trudell said his client, who had no previous convictions, had instructed him to 'apologize to the court and the Toronto community and to say he would also like to commend the police officer who arrested him for his courtesy and polite manner'.

After fining Gibson $C300 and suspending his driver's licence for three months, Judge Carter closed the case with the words: 'I hope your stay in Canada is otherwise pleasant.'

It wasn't all that pleasant though. *Mrs Soffel* was a difficult film to make, conditions were harsh, and Gibson was missing his wife and family who had returned to Australia after several weeks in Toronto. He was tired, frequently cold, sometimes hung over and often lonely.

Mrs Soffel was based on a true story, an extraordinary tale of frustration, repression and infatuation played out in 1901. Kate Soffel (Diane Keaton) was the wife of the warden of the Allegheny County Jail in Pittsburgh. A Christian, compassionate and caring, she did much welfare work among prisoners who included the Biddle brothers, Ed (Gibson) and Jack (Mathew Modine), sentenced to be hanged for murdering a grocer during a burglary. Kate became attracted to Ed who skilfully played on her emotions until she agreed to help him and his brother escape. She brought him a hacksaw and being a Christian, used a Bible to smuggle it into jail. The Biddles escaped, accompanied by Mrs Soffel, but were tracked down in a tragic ending.

The escape both delighted and scandalized Pittsburgh. Here were all the ingredients of fine melodrama with the newspapers running their own commentary. From the *Pittsburgh Leader* of 1901: 'The Biddle brothers, the most notorious murderers in history, escaped from County Jail this morning. Mrs Peter K. Soffel, the wife of the jail warden, is missing and all evidence obtainable seems to tend to the theory that she assisted in the escape. Is Mrs Soffel demented? The capture of the fugitives is in very grave doubt . . .'

The story appealed to Gillian Armstrong, the Australian director who had made a considerable name for herself with *My Brilliant Career* and *Starstruck*. Hollywood had been after her for some time without success. 'I was sent hundreds of scripts and I wasn't interested in any of them,' said Armstrong. 'Diane Keaton, with whom I had become good friends, sent me a book and two screenplays she wanted me to direct, but I turned them down. Then along came *Mrs Soffel* and there was something about it that intrigued me. Here was a woman who had taken a risk with her life. She sacrificed the lot for love and I admire her for taking that chance. I believe in people following their instincts. I spent a weekend with Diane and we talked about the screenplay. It was then I knew I wanted to do it and so did she.'

Armstrong had her leading lady. Her leading man was less easy to snare. She wanted Mel Gibson but he was receiving the full Hollywood treatment: that is, he was protected by layers of people whose main task was to make access as difficult as possible. Armstrong told writer Deborah Tarrant of her problems: 'In America, Mel has no competition as the new leading man. He has two attributes above all the alternatives in the same age group: he has great charisma on screen and he can act. I don't think anyone here [Australia] realizes what a star Mel is in America. I mean, you don't screen test Mel. It is a hoo-ha to even have lunch with him. He's living in hotels under assumed names. His agents even wanted us to enter a restaurant by the back door. I refused. Mel has been offered the male lead in every major American film in the last eighteen months. He's a serious actor, and he's very choosy. I'm just lucky he likes the script and is willing to take a chance with me.'

Armstrong's account suggested Gibson had his career mapped out, that he knew his next move, that nothing was a surprise. It was not that way at all. Gibson himself dismissed the notion that his life was a series of carefully marked charts. 'I never planned a career,' he said at the time of making *Mrs Soffel*. 'I still don't. It kills people when I tell them this, but I don't have a master plan. I just take things as they come, flow with it, go with my gut instincts – or sometimes go against them. You have to know when to do that too.'

Diane Keaton, Mel Gibson and Matthew Modine star in the true story of a prison warden's wife who helps two prisoners to escape in the powerful, romantic drama. *Mrs Soffel*. (© MGM/UA/Jean Pagliuso)

Paul Mansfield, a reporter trying to get an interview with Gibson on location in Toronto, also came slap bang against the wall Hollywood had built around Gibson. These walls are curious structures because on the one hand Hollywood craves publicity, on the other is almost frightened of the media. Furthermore, the walls are sometimes built without the star's knowledge. The star wonders why he hasn't been interviewed for a while, thus increasing his insecurity and the income of Beverly Hills psychiatrists, not knowing that a minder is keeping away reporters like they were summons-servers. Little wonder the writer Ben Hecht was moved to say: 'Many ironic things happen in Hollywood. Overnight, idiots become geniuses and geniuses become idiots, waitresses turn into duchesses and what duchesses turn into won't bear mentioning. Overnight, in Hollywood, panhandling hams blossom into Coquelins and Lorenzos and vice versa. The boulevards are crowded with royal coaches turning into pumpkins before your eyes. It's an Aladdin's lamp of a town, and whichever way you rub it, genii jump out and make sport of the laws of gravity and sanity.'

For almost two months Paul Mansfield tried to breach the wall around Gibson, doing the rounds of studio secretaries, public relations firms and personal assistants. He learned that studio people like to use phrases such as 'output quality' and 'exposure ratio' and refer to their property by his first name only, even if they've never met him, which could be confusing if you're wishing to contact Tom Cruise and not Hanks or Selleck.

Finally, Mansfield tracked Gibson down to what he described as 'a small location unit deep in the snowdrifts north of Toronto'. But before the interview he was told what questions he could or could not ask.

'Mel gets sick of people asking him about politics and stuff,' said one public relations man. 'After all, why does he have to have an opinion on anything?'

By now Mansfield was wondering if Mel Gibson even had a brain. He figured Gibson's handlers were keeping him away so no one would realize he'd become seriously unhinged.

Mansfield was pleasantly surprised therefore to find an amiable Gibson sitting on his couch in his mobile trailer, pleased he had an afternoon off work due to a snow thaw. He seemed puzzled when Mansfield told him of his experiences in trying to set up an interview.

'I don't understand it,' he said. 'It's true that I've narrowed the publicity side down. I did three straight months of it nearly, you know, and I finally got jack of it. But I've got publicity agents now, people like that.'

'I know you have,' Mansfield said. 'And I've spoken to all of them.'

Gibson laughed. 'Well, at least you know what it's like to get that kind of attention.'

To be fair, Gibson was co-operative with those reporters who managed to penetrate the Hollywood wall during the making of *Mrs Soffel*. He told one reporter he accepted the role in *Mrs Soffel* 'because I was drawn to the romantic nature of the story. It's the right mixture of realism and romanticism, and in this case the realism supports the romanticism. And everybody wants a romance . . . To me sex appeal means they want to go and watch what I'm doing – and that's good. But you are not going to get to people, ultimately, by ripping your clothes off and showing them your frontals. It's got to come from here.' He tapped his head. 'You have to gain their respect.'

But during the interview he showed the doubts, the fears, the concern about tomorrow that niggled away at the otherwise comfortable life of the star. The feeling was never far below the surface, ready to pop up at any moment like a pimple. 'I'll probably be washed out in a couple of years,' he confessed. 'People get tired of seeing your face. They want to see another face. And there are faces better and there are talents better – or as good.'

Gibson worked on *Mrs Soffel* in conditions that often could be described only as gruelling. A major scene involved a chase between horse-drawn sleighs across endless snow. A flash heatwave melted the snow and just as the studio granted permission for a costly change of location, a freak blizzard trapped the crew.

'One scene alone took me a full week to get in the camera,' said Armstrong. 'It was the most exhausting sequence I've ever directed and I never want to do a snow scene like that again.'

There was the problem of the crew leaving footprints in the snow. Each footprint, every mark made by vehicles, had to be filled in and swept. At times conditions were too dangerous for filming outside, forcing the cast and crew into a refrigerated warehouse so that the actors' icy breath would still be visible. And all the time the studio back in Hollywood was nagging Armstrong about delays, costs, everything a director would rather not think about when trying to create a story on film.

Not all Gibson's time in Canada was spent sitting in a trailer surrounded by snow drifts, or even driving along Yonge Street. One day he met Dyson Lovell, a British actor turned producer, and they went to the house Gibson was then occupying. Lovell was impressed when he noticed the complete works of Shakespeare lying on the kitchen table. 'We started doing speeches from various plays and carried on well into the evening,' Lovell said. 'He was word-perfect on some of the sonnets.'

Dyson Lovell never forgot the meeting. Several years later he would be responsible for getting together the budget for *Hamlet*.

From Canada the crew moved to Pittsburgh to film the original Allegheny County Jail, still used today, a melancholy building designed in 1883 to resemble a large, fortified church. After much discussion and passing of money, prison authorities had agreed the jail could be used, along with fifty inmates wearing the striped uniforms of the period, and a dozen guards.

Prisoners thought playing prisoners was a splendid notion. Even though they had to cut off their beards and hair because in 1901 it was short back, sides and top, almost five hundred stepped forward to fill the fifty places, anxious for more than the routine of laundry, making licence plates or planning their next crime.

'I picked a good time to come to jail,' said inmate Larry Lindsay, doing ten months for burglary and criminal conspiracy. 'I'm a jack of all trades. I did a little bit of carpentry and a little bit of welding before I went to jail, but I never did any acting. I figure it can't hurt to learn.'

He didn't learn a lot. None of the prisoners were likely to be nominated for an Academy Award. Lindsay and the others did little more than wander in the background, just milling around and mumbling to themselves, as prisoners always have.

Then filming was over. Everyone was relieved, especially Mel Gibson. 'I've pigged out,' he said. 'I'll go home and take a nap.'

He didn't nap for long. Within three months he was making his next movie which while a professional triumph was a personal disaster.

9
Return of Mad Max

Coober Pedy is a lousy place to make a movie. There are probably more uncomfortable locations – Death Valley and the Sahara come to mind – but not many. Some 900 kilometres north west of Adelaide in the rocky Stuart Range, Coober Pedy lies barren and dusty and pitted with the shafts of opal mines, giving it the appearance of a moonscape. The temperature freqently goes above forty degrees, the wind howls, the dust swirls, the flies swarm, the throat dries, the eyes hurt, the sun fries the brain.

But it doesn't stop the search for the milky white opal, first discovered in 1915. Nothing stops the belief that this could be the day a fortune will be revealed. The miners drill shafts into the rock, blast tunnels, pick and gouge in search of potch, or opal colour, their entire lives dictated by the harsh conditions. Many live in underground houses cut from the rock, comfortable if claustrophobic abodes of three or four rooms. There is an underground church and an underground motel and a thousand underground secrets hinted at only occasionally when the booze flows at the pub.

'Haven't seen old Jack around, have you?'

'Nah, reckon he's shot through.'

'Not Jack. Someone's done him in.'

'Wouldn't be the first. Won't be the last.'

In the main street of Coober Pedy, in front of a straggle of shops and cafés, the miners' trucks are parked, many carrying a sign warning that they have explosives on board. The old movie theatre had a notice asking miners to refrain from bringing explosives inside. They use explosives like

Mad Max returns – with Tina Turner in *Beyond Thunderdome*
(© Kennedy Miller)

kids might use crackers and laugh when they recall the stick of gelignite dropped down the air shaft of a miner's underground house. It landed on his stove, but he managed to flee before his stew was blown all over the room.

The miners are a tough breed with no past: independent, secretive, wary of all strangers because the tax man comes in a thousand disguises. All they have in common besides optimism is a respect for the lunar landscape around them. They know it can kill.

So it's a lousy place to make a movie. But, of course, ideal as a location for the return of Mad Max. After all, the story of *Mad Max Beyond Thunderdome* has the hero in a post-holocaust landscape, a blasted and dismembered wasteland, and if there was one thing Coober Pedy could provide other than opals it was such a setting.

The *Mad Max* producers, Kennedy Miller, originally had no intention of making a third movie about the dark and lonely figure Mel Gibson had introduced to the world, just as they had had no intention of making a second. After *Mad Max II*, its creators, George Miller and Terry Hayes, stood beside a road in Broken Hill, where the film was made, shook hands and agreed the end had come.

But there was huge pressure from Hollywood for a third film because of the astonishing successes of the first two. Both made on small budgets, they had grossed so much at the box office they were legends in a Hollywood grown tired and soft and empty of fresh ideas and which could see no further than the cash register. Hollywood's thinking was (and for that matter still is) when in doubt make a sequel.

'I never set out to make a trilogy,' Miller said. 'I tried to develop other subjects, but always Mad Max would emerge. . . . Terry Hayes and I were working on another script. We went out to dinner one night and started to discuss a story about a lost tribe of kids. We started with these kids and they served to bring Max out of the closet a bit, make him more human.'

Warner Bros came up with $A12 million (£5.5 million), a huge leap from the $A4 million budget for *Mad Max II* and the pittance of $A400,000 for *Mad Max I*. A tempting bait was dangled in front of Gibson, who was not especially keen to don the leather and the scars of the character for the third time. The first time he played Mad Max he was paid $A15,000, the second $A120,000. For his third effort he was offered $A1,200,000. He accepted.

Rock singer Tina Turner was signed as Aunt Entity, a part that required her to wear a chain mail costume weighing 32kg in the heat of Coober Pedy. It was an inspired choice, prompting one reviewer to comment: 'Aunt Entity has all the exotic command of the demon-woman, with a touch of the psychotic humour so essential to Mad Maxian style.'

At an old brick works in Sydney sets were constructed, including the medieval-looking village of Bartertown and Underworld – a subterranean industrial complex fuelled by methane gas derived from pig shit. 'It's the first attempt in cinematic history to use four hundred pigs in a dramatic role,' said Terry Hayes.

But it was at Coober Pedy that the spectacular desert scenes were shot. Conditions were appalling. At one stage seven crew members were taken to hospital with heat exhaustion. Tempers frayed. Frustrations boiled. Some of the stunts were so dangerous that, after one particularly scary sequence, a burly stuntman was heard to mutter: 'That's it. I'm going back to the dress shop.'

To this desolate, forsaken land came Mel Gibson, mentally and physically tired, worried about his career, and drinking too much.

Some years later, his drinking under control, he was able to look back with a clinical eye on the days of *Mrs Soffel* and *Mad Max Beyond Thunderdome* when his hand was never far from a beer can. He was able to see that at one stage his life was a blur. 'Not drinking certainly does make a difference to the tenor of my work. When you stop your mind clears up a little, you're able to see things a little more clearly. Even one drink stays in your spine for months . . . it's amazing how it can affect you . . . you don't realize it. I just don't let it become a big habit again.'

The US magazine *People* visited him on the set and found him slumped and sullen and distinctly unhappy. 'I don't want to be doing this interview,' Gibson told the reporter. 'I don't even want to be making this film. Don't print that.'

His next comments perhaps showed something of the turmoil inside him. 'It's all happening too fast. I've got to put the brakes on or I'll smack into something.' Then he went on to blame the press for his problems: 'It's as if you have your pants down around your ankles and your hands tied behind your back. So it's a good opportunity for some parasite to come up and throw darts in your chest.'

Mel Gibson, 'owner of the country's most kissable lips' makes the traditional handprint in cement at the fortieth Cannes Film Festival in 1987.

To make matters worse, *People* dubbed him The Sexiest Man Alive, a title he neither wanted nor welcomed and one that would nag him like a toothache. He would later be bestowed with other vacuous titles – one of the ten most watchable men in America and owner of the country's most kissable lips – but by then he had learned to live with such nonsense.

He worked hard under the blazing sun but the elaborate stunts left him plenty of time to wait around playing cards, drinking beer, smoking cigarettes, telling jokes, talking. Plenty of time to brood. At first the stunt performers, or stuntees as they liked to be called, with whom Gibson mixed freely, could find no chink in his armour. Not at first. But with a gruelling four-month shoot, the chinks would appear one by one.

Gibson had learned from his court appearance during the making of *Mrs Soffel* that drinking and driving are not looked on with amusement by law enforcement agencies. The producers of *Thunderdome* provided him with a driver and a minder so that for their star there would be no blurred drives through red traffic lights, no pedestrians to steer around, no cops flashing lights in his face.

Gibson was not a drunk. Nor was he an alcoholic. But he was putting away too much grog and his voice was becoming raspier because of too many cigarettes. Never a problem on the set, he acted his role with complete control and assurance, was always on time and knew his dialogue (not that there was an awful lot to learn). He was the complete professional.

Some of the stunt team told him he had aged, that he looked haggard and tired. He defended himself, shaking his head and saying: 'It's part of my character for the movie.'

But those close to him knew that wasn't it. He was tired and unsure of himself in a way he had never been before. *The Year of Living Dangerously* had given him a chance to display his acting ability. But the movie hadn't set the world on fire. Then came three box office flops. *The Bounty*, *The River* and *Mrs Soffel*. Gibson, his agents and his mates knew that unless *Thunderdome* did good business he was in danger of being washed up at twenty-nine.

Gibson had created his own demons but he began blaming others, especially the media. 'They're just looking for headlines when there aren't any,' he told movie director and writer Terry Bourke.

In return, some reporters who had known Gibson for several years, who had promoted him, drunk with him, and enjoyed his company, began to question his attitude. They were suggesting Gibson was on a roller-coaster ride to oblivion.

'The desert heat has got to him,' one journalist said in a radio interview. 'He's a different guy. I don't think he even knows himself now.'

One of the reasons he turned on the press was his concern for his mother, Anne. She would read the stories of his hell-raising and, like any mother, worried over them. Some stories were untrue but there were enough of them floating around like bad smells to suggest that her son was either going off the rails or needed a new press agent.

'I never chastised him about it but he knew how I felt,' she said shortly before her death in December 1990. She believed her son found instant fame hard to handle and that that caused his drinking problem. 'Mel was tired and confused and missed the family. It was a matter of priorities. It didn't take him long to sort them out. He's always been like that.'

Referring to his arrest for driving under the influence during the making of *Mrs Soffel*, Anne Gibson said: 'That really woke Mel up. He realized he'd let the beer take hold. The boy changed after that. I was particularly happy no one got hurt in the transition. It could have been tragic.'

During his despairing days Gibson even asked one leading show business writer how he could arrange for 'better press . . . these latest incidents really hurt my ladies. Robyn knows me too well, and she's a big help. But poor old mum freaks out and really suffers when she reads anything I've done, whether it's true or not. I'm not really like I'm made out to be, am I?'

The stuntees became increasingly concerned about Gibson. Independent, tough, sometimes rough, always fiercely loyal, they are virtually unknown to the public, but they are the performers who can make or break a picture like *Thunderdome*. They liked Gibson because he was their sort of person, completely lacking in bullshit, funny, dedicated. Furthermore, he wasn't frightened of doing stunts himself. Not the real hard ones, not falling from a window or getting blown up, but willing to go where many macho actors were afraid to tread. But now he was looking like a guy who had gone too many rounds with Saturday night. Noting the way he was heading, they listened to him as he talked about his career, the failures, the future. Maybe listening could help.

'Mel had always been one of the boys, especially with us stuntees,' one told Terry Bourke. 'He's usually like a brother, but lately, man, the booze has got to him. It's like he's too much into the Mad Max character.'

Sydney-based stuntman Frank Lennon, who died in 1989 after accidentally falling ten feet from a balcony – a miserable death for a man who had made a living out of falling – said, after the completion of *Thunderdome*, that Gibson was haunted by the box office failure of his three previous movies. He felt that he and his agents could not have made three mistakes in a row and spent a lot of time trying to determine what had gone wrong.

Said Lennon: 'He wouldn't accept the basic logic we offered. "Hell, Mel, no one wanted to see the damn things. Word of mouth killed the three of those flicks. Not you. Not your performance." And he'd agree, for about ten minutes. Then he'd analyse it all from a money point of view. Not his money, the cost of the film.

'Mel would counter by saying, "Look at the budgets, man, the leading ladies, the directors. . . . Class, man, class. . . . *River* was a top story. It deserved better. . . . *Mrs Soffel*, well, maybe they don't like the main characters getting shot up at the end. . . . Diane [Keaton] was great, wasn't she?"'

While Gibson was acting and brooding and wondering if, hell, it was all worth it, the South Australia police were planning a drug raid. Gibson was one of their targets. Now it should be pointed out that alcohol and nicotine were Gibson's drugs, nothing else. 'Mel wasn't into it, and steered clear of guys who were,' said Frank Lennon. 'If he had a drug, it was those bloody cigarettes.'

But the police had been tipped off – falsely, as it turned out – that if they raided the movie people at Coober Pedy they could well catch Gibson. It would be a great catch, a prize, good for publicity. The police forces of the world have thought along these lines ever since they nabbed Mick Jagger for possessing a smidgin of dope, and Robert Mitchum before him.

So one day a squad of cops left Adelaide for Coober Pedy. There were some drugs being used by people making the movie, a little cocaine, some marihuana, but nothing like the excesses on many American pictures. In particular, the stunt team couldn't afford to be as stoned as an American Embassy;

their lives depended on their brain knowing what their body was doing.

The cops were only forty-five minutes from Coober Pedy when crew and cast were tipped off that the law was on its way, allowing ample time to clear away illegal substances. One stuntman was charged, but later the case against him was dismissed. Disappointed by their lack of a haul, especially one containing a big name, the cops repaired to the local pub to escape the heat and quench their thirst and conclude they were no closer to promotion.

Filming continued in Sydney for the Bartertown sequences and in the Blue Mountains, on the outskirts of Sydney, where it was as cold as Coober Pedy had been hot. Again Gibson did some of his own stunts, including the scene where Max fights for his life in the *Thunderdome* while bouncing on the end of a bungee rope. 'Mel moved better than the stunt extras, so we decided to let him do the bumps and scrapes himself,' said director George Miller. 'It was safe, just physically demanding. When it was over he was worn but fit.'

The movie completed, the hype began. Tina Turner was asked if she was attracted to Mel Gibson. 'The guy is very married, no playing around,' she said. 'Anyway, he's not really my type. I'm sorry I can't tell the girls he's a great lover. But he's a wonderful person, jolly and not a contrived actor.'

Mel Gibson wasn't saying anything. He had retired to his property near Tangambalanga to recover from too many movies and too much fame too soon.

'It was a scary thing, all that attention,' he later told reporter Karen Milne. 'And there was too much work involved. My career wasn't doing well because I was doing it for the wrong reasons, you know, just knocking off one film after another. That's not why I started. I started because I enjoyed it, and I wasn't enjoying it. I was sick of everything, I couldn't have kept working even if I wanted to.'

He spent time with his family, rode the paddocks, breathed the fresh air, worked hard, talked to locals who couldn't have cared less about *Mad Max*. And maybe he remembered his childhood when his father taught him the Ten Commandments.

'Now I'm going to tell you the eleven,' Hutton Gibson had said. 'Thou shalt not kid thyself.'

10

Onwards and Upwards
'Lethal Weapon'

Mel Gibson spent eighteen months on his property, not only recharging his batteries but re-evaluating his attitude to the business of making movies. *Mad Max Beyond Thunderdome* had turned out to be a huge box office success. His career was not only saved but considerably boosted. His agents received scripts almost daily. Some of the biggest directors and producers in Hollywood were anxious to have his signature on the end of a million-dollar contract. The film world was at his feet.

The eighteen months away from films had been vital, not only for his physical health but also for his mental wellbeing. 'I felt I had to clear my head,' he said. 'It took nearly a year for me to get my straitjacket off. I didn't know what to do with all the attention I had been getting. It was confusing and I needed time to see where I went wrong. I was starting to slip, I had to learn to relax and not take things in Hollywood too seriously. I realized you had to put on the brakes or go away and return to the fray with new armour.'

He looked hard at his relationship with the media, that until then had not been warm. Frigid would be a better description. Concluding that the media were not really so bad and that they were a part of the business he was in, he decided some give and take might not be out of order. In no time at all he was chatting to reporters like they were old pals.

'I used to be afraid of this,' he said to one reporter, looking at the tape recorder whirring between them. 'Now it's not worth getting worried about.'

To another he said: 'This time last year I could never sit down and talk to complete strangers about myself the way I'm doing now. But I've emerged as a new bold me. I've decided that life's too short.'

He was able to handle press conferences with relative ease. To say he was completely comfortable, that he sat there cracking jokes and telling funny stories like a Peter Ustinov, would be an exaggeration, but he was able to speak for longer than half a sentence and even to discuss the price of fame.

'When you're just living your life as normal and you walk down the street and nobody notices, and then all of a sudden that (being noticed) begins to happen, it's not a natural way to exist,' he told a press conference. 'You are not used to it and you think it's going to be great. But it's not. . . . And then when that happens you can go two ways. You can kind of try and kill it. It becomes a problem that you can try and wrestle and fight with, right, just fight it, just be ill at ease with it, and you usually end up in a lot of trouble that way. So what you've got to do is ignore it, in a way, but not be fighting it and it'll just be water off a duck's back. I think it's something that you have to get to, it's stages of . . . it's hard to explain.'

He may have been more at ease but he was no better at constructing sentences. Still, he was giving it a go. He was making up for the bad times. At another press conference he agreed he had a reputation for hating interviews. 'True,' he nodded. 'I suppose I thought I'd make an idiot of myself. I used to build up a lot of negative energy about doing them. I guess it's like cheesecake. If somebody told you about a cake made of cheese and you'd never had it, you'd think it was terrible. Now I've been doing this for a while and I've got used to it.'

He cut down on drinking. He was soon able to tell Sydney show business writer Matt White that he had not touched a drop of alcohol for eight months. 'When my doctor told me my liver was shot to hell, I decided it was time to quit drinking,' he said. 'The first month was awful, but now I'm happy to drink just soda water.'

With his agents, Gibson sorted through the scripts that were arriving almost as frequently as his fan mail. He had knocked back the chance to play James Bond, describing the character as 'kind of boring'.

The script they liked best carried the title *Lethal Weapon*. After some negotiations, Gibson flew to Hollywood, a town he once described as 'a

Mel Gibson and Richard Donner, director of *Lethal Weapon* and *Lethal Weapon II*, Sydney 1987 (© Michael Jones, News Ltd)

great place – to stay away from', and met with director Richard Donner. At Donner's home he was joined by Danny Glover, who was to be his co-star, and together they went through a few lines from the script to see if any chemistry existed between them. 'It became apparent there was something happening,' said Glover.

Gibson said he had 'warmed to Glover almost immediately we met before the rehearsals. We spent a lot of time together. Had some real fun at readings. Then, once we got it together before the cameras, it was spot on, like clockwork . . . he's a great talent to bounce off.'

Gibson signed to play the part of Martin Riggs, a Vietnam veteran now a Los Angeles cop, who is suicidal following the death of his wife. To get the feel of what a cop must face, he and Glover went out on patrols with the Los Angeles Sheriff's Department. Gibson found it was a tough, dangerous and exhausting way to make a living. A cop goes to work with the thought that this could be the last day of his life.

'It's hard to imagine what it's like to be a policeman until you find yourself in that situation,' Gibson said. 'You feel very vulnerable. I was never involved in anything big. They obviously weren't going to throw me into the middle of the hotspot in LA. But it's just your whole perception – and your imagination starts to get to you. You even start to look at little old ladies walking along the street in a different way. You can see why these guys are wired up and ready for action all the time. You can also see why they have a lot of problems in the police force. There are many marriage break-ups, a high suicide rate. I gained a lot of respect for them . . . I'd hate to do it. It must be terribly hard and you don't get many rewards for it.'

At first Richard Donner was wary of Gibson. 'I was expecting to have problems with him,' he confessed. 'I thought he was going to be a method actor, somebody who wanted to know where everything came from and why. But give him one word and he runs with it. Half the time he doesn't even need that.'

Donner was soon to find that in Gibson he had more than an actor. He had someone who could add dimensions to a character that were not in the script, could give that little extra that is the difference between a good performance and one that lights up the screen. He found this out in an important scene where a despondent Martin Riggs puts his police revolver in his mouth and slowly starts to squeeze the trigger, a common

Mel Gibson with patients at Royal Children's Hospital, Sydney, 1987
(© Barry McKinnon, News Ltd)

form of suicide among stressed-out police. The author, Joseph Wambaugh, a former Los Angeles cop, calls it 'smoking the .38'.

'It was a fantastic highlight of the film and came up early in the first reel,' Donner told Terry Bourke. 'Because the scene was so intense, and shot under extremely difficult cramped conditions inside a trailer van, only the camera operator was in the van with Mel as he went through his paces. I checked the revolver myself before it was handed to Mel by the unit's official armourer. Even a blank would inflict terrible damage if it went off when the barrel was near his mouth. (Wadding from a blank killed actor Jon Erik Hexum during a studio lunch break on the set of his series, *The Hunter*.)

'I watched the scene on a video monitor outside the van. I watched . . . I couldn't believe what Mel was doing. It was so real. I thought, hell, he might have put a shell in the gun . . . things rushed through my head. Did Mel ask the armourer or special effects guy to "put one in there to give me motivation"? I tell you, I was terrified as Mel started to choke on the barrel, his finger tightening on the trigger. I was torn between rushing in and stopping the scene in case there was a shell in the gun and getting this amazing performance. I was literally glued to watching the video screen. The crew was spellbound. A couple of the girls were choking, beginning to cry behind me.

'I figured we had what we wanted and was about to call "cut" into the radio mike that went to the cameraman's earphones. But Mel kept it going, adding a few final tears of frustration and mental anguish as he wept openly, apologizing to a photo of his dead wife. I can tell you I breathed out loud when he stopped the performance and I called a meek "cut" to the operator.

'I rushed into the van and hugged Mel. Told him it was great, fantastic. He looked around, shook his head. "Want to try another one, for safety?" he said to me quite innocently, wiping a real tear from his eye.

'I gave him another hug and said, "You were perfect, the film gate is clear. We've got it."

'I could never have gone through that again. But Mel would have done it again, gladly. When I saw the scene intact as part of the finished film it still took my breath away. My hair stood on end. This sort of thing rarely happens. With Mel I guess anything is possible. He's one of the greats and he seems to be cruising most of the time.'

Mel's performance in the gun-in-mouth scene was so chillingly realistic that in cinemas voices screamed from the audience: 'No, don't . . . don't do it.'

Mel Gibson and Danny Glover star in *Lethal Weapon*. (© Warner Bros. Inc.)

Across the world another person was later to see the scene and not only be deeply moved but make a decision that would startle many in the film business. The great Italian director, Franco Zeffirelli, was so impressed with Gibson's performance, he made a mental note to talk to the actor. As he said later to Christopher Day, for the Australian publication *TV Week*: 'There was a scene in which he has a kind of "to be or not to be" speech with a gun. But he's not able to pull the trigger. When I saw that I said, "Zees ees Hamlet. Zees boy ees Hamlet! Bong! Bing!"'

But that was further down the track. Right then Gibson was involved in *Lethal Weapon*: it is a violent film and Martin Riggs is a violent man. 'Have you ever met anyone you haven't killed?' his partner, Roger Murtagh, asks.

Realizing that too much violence can become oppressive, Gibson at times improvised and injected humour into his character with throw-away lines. 'I wanted to give the character a bit of life,' he explained. 'I thought that to give a man who was in so much pain a bit of light relief would be interesting. I got the idea from a Shakespearean play.'

Gibson does have an appealing sense of humour. He is noted on film sets for his antics, his practical jokes, his bad puns. It's as though there's a comic inside him struggling to get out. But the characters he had played until Martin Riggs did not allow much room for humour. Mad Max was not a funny man, nor was Fletcher Christian noted for his comic performances.

People who have worked with Gibson have mentioned his sense of humour.

'He could have been a Marx brother, there's something undeniably zany about the man,' said Robert Towne, who directed him in *Tequila Sunrise*. 'Beneath the romantic exterior, there is this preposterous farceur longing to get out.'

Said Richard Donner: 'Mel Gibson is God's gift to a director. But he tells the worst jokes in the world.'

Added Sigourney Weaver: 'He can sing and dance and he's all over the place, and he's very funny. Mel is all the Three Stooges rolled into one.'

Gibson admitted he 'liked to horse around. And I figure if you have to work for a living, you might as well make fun of it. What I do certainly isn't a cure for cancer. And one of the best things about this job is that you can enjoy yourself at it almost all the time.'

Before filming of *Lethal Weapon* began, Gibson got his body into shape by lifting weights and training in martial arts. He needed to be fit, especially for the climactic scene in which he fights the villain, played by Gary Busey, on the front lawn of Roger Murtagh's house. 'Yeah, it was a hell of a scene,' Gibson said. 'Water pouring from a burst main, hovering helicopter with its blinding light, cop cars and uniformed cops everywhere, chanting for Riggs to "kill the bastard".

'Sure, Gary and I had some stunt guys doing a couple of the really hairy moves. But, when we finished the scene, after four days of being so wet I could feel every sore bone in my body. It was like I'd been run over by a bus. But when I watched the rushes the next night I knew it would all come together as a great final piece. I felt it was all worth it, even though the bones still creaked.'

A sequel was inevitable. In fact, a sequel had been decided on before the shooting was finished. 'Halfway through the film Dick (Donner) told us we were going to end up with a biggie . . . he didn't say how big, but the studio guys were already talking about a sequel,' said Gibson.

Lethal Weapon eventually grossed around $A260 million (£120 million). Mel Gibson could now virtually write his own ticket. Hollywood had already decided he was the next great matinee idol.

Before starting his next picture, *Tequila Sunrise*, Gibson returned to his Australian property. He had learned that to make one movie after another, as he had in the days of *The River* and *Mrs Soffel*, was dangerous. The body and mind had to be rested.

Gibson liked the *Tequila Sunrise* script the moment he read it. 'I was intrigued as soon as I started reading it, although I didn't understand it – "Just be patient; eventually, it'll pay off." It's one of those things that sucks you in slowly, but surely,' Gibson told *Prevue* magazine.

Gibson was also keen to work with Robert Towne, who was something of a legend in Hollywood after his Oscar for the private eye classic, *Chinatown*.

But there was one problem with Gibson's character Dale (Mac) McKussic. He was a former drug dealer, no longer in the business, but living comfortably from the proceeds of distributing cocaine. Gibson knew he would have to tread carefully, as he explained on an American breakfast show while promoting the movie: 'Look, no one's perfect, and most of us have done something in life we regret or may even be ashamed of. I felt the character of McKussic was legitimate. He wasn't pushing any more; he saw the future of his son as more important than his own or his past. I mean, sure, he dealt in drugs . . . but when the story opens he's been clean.

'Personally, and it's well known publicly, I detest drugs, hate the damn things . . . I won't go near them, and I would hate to think my kids or

With Michelle Pfeiffer and Kurt Russel as ex-drug dealer 'Mac' McKussic in *Tequila Sunrise*. (© Warner Bros. Inc.)

anyone's kids could get hooked on them. We are the ones that make sure they don't get hit.'

Even as he was talking, Gibson had a drug problem of his own. He was hooked on nicotine. He had tried to give up his habit of lighting up Marlboros. 'The other day,' he told *Prevue* magazine, 'one of my kids came up, saw me smoking and said, "Please don't. I don't want you to die." They really believe that if I have another one, I could drop dead on the spot. And I could. That's a pretty strong motivation to quit.'

When he had finished his little speech to the interviewer, he picked up a packet of Marlboro, planted a cigarette in his mouth, set fire to it and inhaled deeply.

In an attempt to get inside the mind of someone who has made a living out of cocaine, Gibson talked to a real drug dealer who had seen the error of his ways after a stretch in jail. 'I'm sure he regretted what he'd done, although he never apologized for it, and never used the stuff himself,' said Gibson. 'He didn't consider the end result; he was just the middleman, exactly like Mac, enjoying the thrill, not to mention the money. . . . He wasn't thinking about the drugs making some kid jump off a roof or shoot his sister. In the film, it's Mac's own little boy who prompts him to rethink his profession.'

Director Towne stoutly defended his film. 'My feeling about this is that the most dangerous thing you can do with that issue is to make *Cocaine Fiends* or *Reefer Madness* (two early anti-drug movies) because then it removes it from the world of reality, and everybody thinks, "Well, I don't have to worry about that. It could never happen in my life." When you show it can be in the context of our normal lives, then you can suggest the damage it does. We can't deal with Dick Tracy kinds of good and evil, because it's just more complicated than that.'

Many reviewers, while conceding Gibson's performance was solid and credible, questioned the drug background of the McKussic character. The comments of Bev Tivey, the highly respected critic for the *Sydney Daily Telegraph*, were typical: 'Can you accept a cocaine dealer as a romantic, lovable, even admirable character, even if he is as handsome as Mel Gibson and is presented as a loyal friend, an ardent lover, a caring father and a connoisseur of food? I'm afraid I can't; though I'm willing when watching a romantic thriller to suspend disbelief and accept all sorts of implausibilities, coincidences and general foolishness, I won't put my moral senses on hold too.'

However, the public didn't seem unduly concerned about the character. *Tequila Sunrise* did nicely at the box office and gave Gibson's career another boost.

11

Encounters with Politics — and Goldie Hawn

Robert Taylor never had a bigger audience. Not the film actor of the same name but an independent candidate in the 1987 Australian federal election, he was used to talking to a few people and a lot of flies. Independent candidates don't draw crowds. Voters are not interested in their minority views because most vote only for three major parties, not some bloke on the back of a truck with a bee in his bonnet about the way the country was going, which according to Taylor was along the road to hell.

Taylor was against many things. He didn't like union power, big government, heavy taxation, Fabian socialism and humanism. What he was for was the family, farmers and small business.

He was twenty-seven, a truck driver from the town of Yarrawonga on the New South Wales–Victoria border. He held some hope he could do well in the elections because in 1987 voters were looking at the three major parties – Labour, Liberal and National – and finding them wanting. They were sick of party politics, of parliamentarians voting, not for the good of the country or their electorate, but the way the party bosses dictated. He thought he might attract the support of disgruntled voters, enough to stir things up a bit and give the major parties a small fright. But a seat in parliament . . . only sometimes did he allow himself to dream the impossible dream.

And yet here he was on the back of a truck in a country showground talking to many more people than the candidates for the three big parties could draw to their meetings. There were about 1,500 gathered around the truck, but a closer look revealed that many were not old enough to vote.

Mel stands up for 'old-fashioned morals and traditional family values' with independent candidate Robert Taylor in the 1987 Australian federal election.

They were, in fact, teenage girls and they clutched autograph books. They didn't want Taylor's autograph. They wanted the signature of his backer. They wanted Mel Gibson's autograph.

Gibson had heard about Taylor's policies, decided they were similar to his own and backed the candidate, not only with money but his physical presence. Which is why there were 1,500 people gathered around a truck on a dusty showground.

'Our nation today is suffering a massive increase in child abuse, drug abuse, suicide, pornography and the AIDS thing,' Taylor thundered. Gibson applauded.

'Our nation is in the grip of hopelessness. That's why you're here today because you're dissatisfied.' This wasn't entirely true. The teenage girls were there for a different reason. Gibson applauded anyway. 'Abortion is legalized mass murder.'

And so it went on. Taylor was pleased with the day's proceedings and especially the attention from the local media. 'I couldn't even get my press releases in the paper before Mel came along,' he said.

Many of the audience were farmers. Some were the daughters of farmers. But they all knew, as did Gibson, the problems and frustration of trying to earn a buck in the country. 'People think these guys sit in their properties in front of their fire and it all just happens,' Gibson said. 'That's crazy. I've never met such hardworking people in my life as I have in the country areas of Australia.'

He didn't make that statement on the day 1,500 gathered at Wodonga showground. He said it a few years later but he felt it, believed it, on the day. And the people sensed he did. Gibson was one of them.

Oddly, Gibson got involved in politics even though he couldn't vote in Australia. He still carried an American passport. He could vote for the president, or the local dogcatcher, back in the United States but in his adopted country of Australia could have no bearing on election results, except by supporting a candidate. 'I haven't got a vote,' he said, around the time word was circulating in the Kiewa Valley that he might be backing a local boy in the national elections. 'But I certainly give a hoot about what's happening to this country, because I'm responsible for bringing six little Australians into the world. I can't think of anything more challenging or important than making sure we can guarantee the future for our young ones.'

Gibson's foray into politics began after chatting to a farming neighbour, Ed Jacobs, who happened to be an advisor and longtime family friend of Taylor.

'He's on the right track,' Jacobs said of Taylor. 'He's running on a platform of old-fashioned morals and a return to traditional family values.'

Mel nodded. They were the values he supported. Gibson may have played some swinging, easy-living characters in his films, oddballs you mightn't want anywhere near your kids, but in the real world he was so conservative he made Ronald Reagan seem a pointy-headed Liberal and Margaret Thatcher a founding member of Friends of the Kremlin.

After hearing what Jacobs had to say Gibson indicated he might be willing to help Taylor's campaign. 'I didn't have the thousands of dollars of campaign funds the other candidates got, we were running on the smell of an oily rag,' said Taylor. 'But Mel believed I was on the right track.'

Taylor flew to Sydney to meet Gibson who was then staying at his Coogee home. Also there was his brother, Donal Gibson. The three men talked amid clouds of cigarette smoke, with Gibson offering coffee and beer and conservative values. The talking broke up for a while, when they all walked to a nearby Chinese restaurant to bring back a meal for the family and themselves, then began again.

'By then Mel was committed to helping me,' said Taylor. 'There were little hints about my wording in speeches, my delivery . . . Mel was great at helping without interfering or treading on toes. I was so lucky having a famous person supporting my own long-held beliefs.

'I learned a lot from that plunge into politics. And quite a lot of it came from watching Mel in action. It wasn't like watching him on screen playing a character. He was speaking from the heart. Mel Gibson the Aussie . . . Mel the father, the family man. He wasn't acting, and the people who came to our campaign meetings knew it too.'

Gibson threw himself into the effort of making his man known, his platform publicized, not only by attending meetings but by driving Taylor's campaign truck around the electorate. On election night they gathered together to watch the results on television. It soon became apparent that not even Gibson could change the in-built attitude of voters who continued to give their support to the established parties. Taylor could snare only nine per cent of the vote. 'Big bucks and the system beat us in the end,' Taylor said.

Taylor disappeared from the political scene, making an honest living instead selling office supplies. However, he did not forsake his dream of political power. He never forgot the day he stood on the back of a truck, Mel Gibson at his side. 'I may run for election to parliament sometime in the future,' he said. 'I've grown, matured and become wiser in the game of politics. But my views are basically intact. I would love to think Mel would be back again. He gave me valuable exposure with solid campaign backing and a grand show of loyalty and convictions but the big bucks and older boys won the day.'

Two years later, at the next federal election, Gibson was back again, this time throwing his weight, influence, charisma and wallet behind another independent candidate, Barry Tattersall, standing in the same electorate of Indi. He went further than before, appearing in television advertisements on the local station chatting with Tattersall about the value of independents in politics.

'He is talking straight from the heart,' Tattersall said of Gibson. 'The value of the individual is important to us and I want to serve the electorate of Indi, not dictate to it.'

Again Mel could not get voters to change their minds. Maybe Martin Riggs or Mad Max could, but, heck, this was Australia, not some half-arsed dictatorship where elections are held at the point of a gun. The voters proved even more conservative than Mel. Voting for an independent was far too radical for them.

The disappointments did not change Gibson's views. He still believed that Australia, and most of the free world, for that matter, was going to hell in a basket. With each birthday he seemed to grow more politically conservative. There wasn't much anyone could teach him about conservatism because he had been taught its virtues since he was old enough to understand what his father was talking about. He could write a book about conservatism, with enough left over for a sequel, another subject he knew about. In the middle of 1990 he appeared on Australian television and told interviewer Ray Martin that he thought politicians were traitors. Pointing out that Australians were battling huge interest rates and taxes, he said: 'I suppose they're going to have a nose-picking tax next. I just don't think the people in power in the Government have in their hearts anything good for the country. I think it's nothing short of traitorous what they're doing.'

He was enthusiastically applauded by the studio audience who seemed generally to agree with former federal cabinet minister, John Brown, who once said: 'Politicians are only two notches above child molesters on the social scale.'

But back to Hollywood . . .

His family ensconced in a Malibu house bought from actor–singer Rick Springfield, Gibson began work on the *Lethal Weapon* sequel. The plot was interesting because a new type of villain was introduced. Hollywood's villains had been Russians, Poles, Hungarians, in other words almost anyone from behind the old Iron Curtain: closer to home there were the Mafia, Colombian drug dealers and, sometimes, the CIA. Now *Lethal Weapon II* introduced South Africans. Furthermore, they were South African consular officials, depicted as being involved in torture, murder and the laundering of narcotic profits.

The South African government took exception and its vice-consul in New York, Paul Bryant, proclaimed that the film was part of a Hollywood trend attempting to promote 'the villainization of South Africa in films. In the film industry, all of a sudden Cuba and the Soviet Union are the good boys. Now they've cast around for another country as a villain and they've picked us.'

But no one was listening. The general opinion was that, considering their record in their own country, South Africans were beyond slander.

The atmosphere on the set in Los Angeles and at San Pedro harbour was warm and funny. Gibson performed even when he wasn't in front of the cameras, walking on to the set wearing coffee filters on his head like a Jewish yarmulke, or bellowing a slightly off-key version of 'Edelweiss' from *The Sound of Music*.

'God, you can't encourage the guy,' said director Richard Donner, walking away giggling after another Gibson jape. 'He tells some awful jokes. But now and then he's very funny, almost hysterical . . . and he laughs like hell himself.'

Encouraged to improvise once again, Gibson threw out lines from the script and added his own, more after than not thought up on the spot. 'You take the situation at hand and see what you find funny and try to introduce it, make it part of the screenplay,' he explained. 'I never improvised as much as I did in this. They give you enough rope to hang yourself and if you do hang yourself they cut it in editing. If it works they leave it in.'

An example of Gibson's ad-lib comedy appeared in the scene where the South Africans prove how despicable they can get by planting a booby trap in Roger Murtagh's toilet. Murtagh [Danny Glover] can't stand up without detonating the bomb, so he has to sit there as forlorn as an orphan bandicoot on a burnt ridge. He is placated by Martin Riggs who stays with him to yank him off the seat at the count of three. They dive sideways to try to minimize the effect of the flying fragments of steel.

After the dust and porcelain clears and the main part of the toilet has been dumped on a police car in front of Murtagh's house, the pair are lying in the wreckage.

Riggs says to Murtagh, their lips only inches apart: 'Come on . . . just a little kiss before they get here.' It was Gibson at his ad-lib best.

One reason for the ad-libs was Gibson's concern that the sequel might not be as successful as the original. 'There's a lot of apprehension attached to sequels,' he said. 'Notoriously, they're never as good as the original. You see a lot of pressure to live up to the standard you've already set. When we first met Riggs, we found him at one of his lowest points. I thought in this film I could take him in a slightly different direction and maybe have some fun.'

His new relaxed attitude ('I'm finally having a good time') extended even to talking about his family, a subject of eternal interest to Hollywood where families seldom increase beyond one before those responsible go separate ways. Not that Hollywood doesn't like big families. Hollywood is continually making movies and television series about families so big they could almost qualify for a seat in the United Nations. Hollywood, however, isn't used to seeing this theme spill from the screen into real life. So Hollywood was fascinated by the Gibson brood. But questions about his family had in the past been answered tersely. His family had nothing to do with his movies; he saw no reason to discuss them in any way.

But reporter Ivor Davis found Gibson willing to talk about the family, even about the dubious joys of changing nappies and how it's important for both child and father, that sort of thing. Gibson sounded like a born-again Dr Spock.

'You have to learn to do that,' he said with a grin. 'I mean, if you walk by and one of the kids needs it done, well, you just can't ignore it, can you? I think there's a kind of bonding that goes on with the kids when that happens. The kid, even if he's just six months old, gets attached to you because you're doing that kind of stuff for him. He doesn't sort of reason it out and say, "Boy, what a great dad he is changing my shitty diaper." But somewhere in the back of his brain it's going to stick with him that you changed his diaper, and stuff like that.'

He admitted it wasn't all fun and games. Dirty nappies are not sacred symbols of the importance of fatherhood. They are merely dirty nappies. 'I really hate the messy ones,' he said. 'But I do 'em because I feel wimpy if I have to call for help. But it's just aaarghhh . . .'

He gave a strangled cry and burst into laughter.

Unlike the original, the *Lethal Weapon* sequel featured Gibson in a love scene, the romance provided by Patsy Kensit, actress and wife of the British keyboard player, Dan Donovan. The scene caused much comment, with many inquisitive souls asking Patsy what it was like to spend the two days of filming in bed with Mel. One magazine boldly displayed the headline: What Patsy Kensit Told Mel Gibson in Bed.

Actually, she didn't tell him anything of great interest. 'I kept whispering in his ear, "God, I miss my husband",' she said.

That wasn't enough for the more salacious newspapers and magazines. Come off it, there must have been more. You had the chance millions of women would kill for, and you reckon you talked about missing your husband. Pull the other one, it's got bells on.

'Okay, it was very weird,' said Patsy reluctantly. 'A very unnatural situation. I mean, he's very married and I'm very married so it felt quite strange to be in bed with someone other than my husband. Before we did the scene, the closest we got to each other was playing Scrabble between takes. The first word I made was "vomit" which he thought was brilliant. Mind you, he did tell me a lot of really dirty jokes   '

And that was about all Patsy Kensit had to say about two days in bed with Mel Gibson. Female fans sighed, C'mon, Patsy, tell us more, but there was no more to tell. In fact, Patsy got a trifle annoyed when the media pressed for extra titillating details. 'I can't see what all the fuss is about,' she snapped.

Although generally well received by critics, *Lethal Weapon II* was attacked by some for its violence. And violent it was, with around thirty deaths depicted: villain decapitated by a surfboard; two others killed by a nail gun; the heroine is drowned; cops are blown up; crooks are shot through the head and any number are smashed to oblivion by Mel's bare hands. An arsenal of weapons is used that could have given Saddam Hussein victory in the Gulf. Blood flows like booze at a publicans' picnic; death is just another way of life.

Gibson answered the criticism in fairly simple terms. 'I don't think the violence is over the top . . . I think you can go too far with violence but we didn't. What we're trying to show is that "We're just kidding, folks". I mean, it's kind of a Three Stooges thing. True, the Three Stooges didn't have semi-automatic weapons, but they had carpentry saws and shoved crowbars in eyes and stuff. It's all an illusion, this violence.'

After *Lethal Weapon II* Gibson went to Canada for his next film, not to Toronto of the bad memories, but Vancouver. He had received all sorts of offers: one a film about motor racing called *Champions*, later to become *Days of Thunder* with Tom Cruise. He was invited to play Robin Hood. He had vague ideas of working on a comedy to be made in Australia. And, of course, any flea-brained producer or director hoping to raise a little money for a movie that wouldn't get off the ground if it was attached to a Saturn rocket, would drop Mel's name like he'd just had lunch with him that day. It would get them some publicity. The telephone would ring for half an hour. That's how Hollywood operates – on rumours.

Gibson, however, had chosen *Bird on a Wire* with Goldie Hawn. He had met Hawn when working with her husband, Kurt Russell, on *Tequila Sunrise*. They became good friends and often discussed making a movie together. Along came the script for *Bird on a Wire*, an ideal vehicle for the pair. 'A frothy piece of fun and action,' as Gibson called it.

The movie was important for Hawn because it had been ten years since her last hit, *Private Benjamin*. Her movies since then, *Wildcats* and *Overboard*, had been flops. Ten years without a hit in Hollywood is about nine years too long. She had everything riding on the success of *Bird on a Wire*.

On the other hand, Gibson was keen to discover how he would come across in a movie without a high body count. The time had come, he reasoned, to display his comic talents to a bigger audience than film crews standing around between shots. 'This is funny and warm,' he said of *Bird*

Mel Gibson and Goldie Hawn in 'a frothy piece of fun and action', *Bird on a Wire*
(© Universal Studios)

on a Wire. 'I've always been afraid to try things like that, but I thought I'd just dive in and see what happened.'

Bird on a Wire is basically a chase movie. Gibson plays a former Sixties radical living a secret life as a government-protected witness after blowing the whistle on two corrupt drug-enforcement agents. Hawn is his former girlfriend who accidentally rediscovers him. So do the bad guys. They chase Gibson and Hawn through a zoo, in cars, on motorcycles, in a plane and aboard a rollercoaster.

Hawn did not like the rollercoaster scenes one bit. So jittery was she that director John Badham limited her scenes to a small section of the track.

Mel Gibson finds himself in a precarious position in *Bird on a Wire*
(© Universal Studios)

'They fork-lifted me up to the rollercoaster like a jackass,' she said. 'I think I risked more doing that than if I had gone on the whole rollercoaster ride. Every fear I've ever had I faced in this movie. I think I'm a new woman now. I can do anything.'

Her main fear was of heights: an inability to stand on anything much taller than the front doorstep without feeling she would topple off. For one stunt she had to climb around the ledge of a twenty storey building, not an easy task for anyone but especially frightening for Hawn. Vertigo took over. She froze, the world started spinning around like a giant turntable and she knew she was going to fall.

But, never fear, Mel was there. As if in a Saturday matinee serial the hero arrived in time. 'Mel grabbed me in his arms and hauled me back,' she said. 'I was shaking and crying. He saved my life.'

Production completed, Goldie Hawn showed she was more than a pretty face scared of heights by plugging the film with tales of bedroom scenes. Movie bedroom scenes, that is. She told reporters eager to hear the worst that she and Mel had had second thoughts about a love scene. 'They were hot and heavy,' Goldie said to the panting press. 'So I got on to Mel and said, "Have you ever seen me do a love scene – it's just not my thing."

'Mel and I agreed that this is not the kind of movie that you do some hot love scenes together. It's a film about love, getting together and remembering. It's innocent. It just wasn't right to see these two people go at it together. It would be a turn-off.'

Even without the hot and heavy love scene, *Bird on a Wire* was able to attract the customers. Gibson now had three box office successes in a row.

12
'Air America' – Thai Style

Deep in the Golden Triangle of Thailand, an area of jungle-clad mountains so steep they make goats nervous, where a soft rain falls for much of the time, where opium poppies bloom in small clearings and drug traders control more firepower than the armourer on *Lethal Weapon*, up there not far from the Burmese border, Mel Gibson felt he might be able to stroll around unrecognized. After all, it was as far from Hollywood as it's possible to go without leaving the planet.

When he had stopped over in Bangkok for a few days before heading north he had been spotted immediately. And not unexpectedly. The Thais are great patrons of the cinema, although preferring movies in the style of *Mad Max* and *Lethal Weapon* to a Fellini masterpiece or something sentimental from Disney. They knew Gibson from the huge billboards in garish colours, some a storey high, scattered around Bangkok, Mad Max staring wild eyed down on the permanent traffic jam that is the city's streets.

Only a few nights before, he had been in a restaurant enjoying the spicy Thai cuisine. Across the room was the rock singer Billy Idol, playing the clown at a table surrounded by an entourage of lesser jesters. A group of teenage girls walked in. Idol preened, his pen poised for an autograph or two, his tongue at the ready for a merry quip. The girls walked past Idol, probably not knowing who he was and seeing just another noisy, round-eyed *farang*, and stopped at Gibson's table. Shyly they asked for his autograph. He obliged by signing paper napkins.

Across at the other table Billy Idol was, according to all reports, fuming. He had been snubbed.

But that's another story and has nothing to do with Gibson in the hill country of Thailand, up north among the tribes – the Karen, the Meo, the Ho – where, for heaven's sake, he would be as anonymous as a priest in St Peter's Square.

He wasn't there a day before people stopped, stared and smiled in his direction. 'Ahh,' they giggled. 'Mad Mack!'

Everywhere he went he was greeted in the same fashion . . . Mad Mack! 'They didn't know what my name was but they knew I was Mad Mack,' Gibson said later, still amused that seemingly there is no place on earth for him to hide. 'That was the thing that really surprised me.'

Gibson was in Thailand to make *Air America*, a saga about the covert airline which the CIA ran out of Laos during the Vietnam War. The real Air America was an extraordinary operation, fuelled by American paranoia and scheduled by a bunch of CIA operatives with fewer scruples than a child molester, or even an Australian politician. They would fly anything around the area, including any amount of top-grade heroin, if they thought it would help in the elimination of another goddamned commie bastard. Or, as Gibson put it: 'Air America flew everything from elephants to opium to monkey embryos. It was amazing. It was the world's biggest airline at one time and you could get anything, anywhere, anytime on these planes.'

Using Air America, the Americans dreamed up some beautiful schemes in an attempt to defeat the enemy. They dropped boxes of oversized condoms behind Vietcong lines in the hope that the enemy would be awed by the size and virility of the American fighting men. Coming from a race that has not heard of penis envy, the Vietcong were far from awed. Rather they were grateful for the condoms because they slipped easily over their rifle barrels, keeping them dry and better equipped to kill young American soldiers.

The pilots themselves were men that in another time might have been buccaneers or western gunslingers. They were brave, tough, skilful and daring. Quite a number were cowboys and not a few were crazy, having lived too long in the area, taken too many substances, seen too many unlikely sights. Southeast Asia can be a white man's asylum.

Originally signed to play the younger pilot, Gibson protested he had 'too many wrinkles to get away with that new-kid stuff anymore'. The part went to Robert Downey Jr. Gibson played Gene Ryack, a world-weary pilot and gunrunner who has found the Laotian way of life to his liking and wants to get out of the business.

Gibson declared he could relate easily to Ryack. 'Born in the USA, he is Captain America but he's been so long away and has become so cynical and jaded that he's Asian on the inside.' Then he drew a bow longer than was ever seen in Sherwood Forest. 'In a way, I'm a bit like that. I was born in the US, moved away and became something else, a creature not of my creation.'

Early in 1990, veteran director Roger Spottiswoode moved into northern Thailand accompanied by fifteen cameras, three units, five hundred crew, twenty-six aeroplanes and helicopters rented from the Thai military, a minder to follow Robert Downey Jr, a physician to treat snakebites and other afflictions better not thought about and a large chunk of the $US35 million (£21 million) budget.

Before shooting could start a few small matters had to be resolved. One of the matters was Khun Sa, the world's biggest smack dealer. Operating on both sides of the Burmese border, Khun Sa controls more than two thousand tons of opium a year. The trade is protected by a well-equipped private army a South American dictator might envy. His men have a habit of taking pot shots at aircraft flying over his region and, because the movie used aircraft the way slapstick uses custard pies, a chance existed one could be shot down, not only irritating the Thai military but playing hell with the film's insurance, not to mention its budget.

Fortuitously, word got back that Khun Sa was a Mel Gibson fan, known to have a collection of *Mad Max* video tapes, and that if the actor wouldn't mind placing his autograph on a piece of paper – he didn't have to write 'To my dear pal, Khun Sa' or anything like that – and sending it by jungle post, everything would be all right. In the parlance of the CIA, the film company never confirmed or denied the tale but it was gospel among film crew and wherever two or three gathered, usually in a bar, it was repeated with enthusiasm. Whatever the truth, not one aircraft suffered from a bullet wound.

When the film company moved to Mae Hong Son, where an airbase out of the Sixties was built, they were in Khun Sa's territory. Maps may have

Mel Gibson plays Gene Ryack, world-weary aviator in *Air America*
(© Greater Union Distributors)

indicated it was included in the sovereign nation of Thailand but everyone knew better. And still no one took pot shots at the film company's hired aircraft.

Into this remote area one day came producer Dan Melnick, aboard a helicopter which had got lost somewhere near the border. Let reporter Robert Sam Anson take up the story as he told it, brilliantly, in *Premiere* magazine: 'On the slope of a mountain they spotted a hill-tribe village. There were ponies, some adorable thatched huts a little smaller than your average pool house, and natives wearing the oddest costumes, black get-ups that it appeared someone back in the Sixties had accessorized with macrame. In a swirl of red dust, the chopper touched down.

'The villagers, who had no contact at all, basically, with the outside world, came out to gape at the insect-like marvel that had landed in their midst. With a screeching clank, its body opened, and a man with frighteningly pale skin emerged. He was clad in a tailored bush-ensemble.

'"Greetings," said Daniel Melnick, offering them a box lunch. "We come from Hollywood."'

Filming in the hills of northern Thailand was, well, different. Whichever way they looked the crew knew they were not in a Hollywood backlot. Gibson described one scene that tickled his sense of humour, if not his palate: 'It was fun, a great deal of fun though it looked tough. The Thais are very hospitable. The guy who managed the place where we stayed – I won't call it a hotel because it was something else – would go down to the river, catch an eight-foot snake, come back, throw it in the pot and eat it.'

Gibson, or Mad Mack, was much sought after by the locals, especially in Chiang Mai, the main town of the hill country, a place popular with tourists seeking a taste of Asian exotica off the beaten track and dope freaks wanting a taste of Khun Sa's acclaimed product. Crowds gathered outside the Arun Rai Chinese restaurant, which in the film became the White Rose café, an establishment remembered fondly by those who frequented it during the Vietnam war. Everything was available at the White Rose, from bar girls to clap, from guns to marijuana carefully rolled and sold in Marlboro packets. The crowds waited patiently while filming went on inside, sometimes asking quietly: 'Mel, u nai, krap? (Where is Mel?)'

A tour operator decided that waiting for Mel was about as profitable as counting raindrops and organized a deal with Gibson's hotel. While the star was filming, the operator took tourists to the hotel, pointed to the closed door of Gibson's room and, in the manner of a guide proudly showing an ancient monument, announced: 'This is Mel Gibson's room!'

Much of the filming at the White Rose was done at night which meant long, tiring hours for the stars and the extras, often ten hours at a stretch. Surprisingly, one of the extras was the United States Ambassador to Thailand, Charles Ray. He hadn't been there long when a reporter wanted to know why a man of his stature, more usually seen at diplomatic cocktail parties, would stay for up to ten hours a night under hot lamps for little pay, especially since the White Rose was an establishment ambassadors would avoid like an international incident.

'I did it to keep peace in my family,' he sighed. 'My thirteen-year-old daughter said if I had a chance to be in a movie with Mel Gibson and I didn't do it, she would never live under the same roof with me again. I figured it better to spend five nights out here in the streets than the next five years with an irate daughter . . .'

As always the actors spent a great deal of time waiting for scenes to be set up. To keep boredom at bay, one night Gibson pretended to be a television reporter and, carrying a video camera, walked into a restaurant where two American couples were dining.

'What brings you to Chiang Mai on a night like this?' he asked, zooming in on one pair.

They looked, swallowed, looked again. My gahd, isn't that . . . no, it can't be . . . not . . .

'Does you wife know you're here with this young woman?' Mel went on.

Gahd, Fred, it is. There were gasps like the impossible was happening before their eyes, here in a restaurant in Chiang Mai in the hill country of Thailand. What a tale to tell the folks back home.

'Hey, you're Mel Gibson.'

Gibson acknowledged it was he. Then he cheerfully posed with the couples for photographs.

Arguably, the busiest man on location was the doctor. As well as warning the crew about AIDS (which has reached plague proportions in Thailand) and about a snake dubbed the two step – 'Coz that's as far as anyone moves after being bitten' – he was working overtime with the hypodermic needle. If there's a disease listed in Black's *Medical Dictionary*, a reasonable chance exists that it has found a home in Thailand. To be on the safe side, the doctor was inoculating for everything. He was even inoculating for a disease carried by baby pigs, as well as dispensing Lomotil like aspirin. But there were still queues outside the lavatories.

'They had mosquitoes there armed with machine guns, it was so bad,' said Gibson. 'We were pumped with so many holes for inoculations I thought I would leak.'

Not only did he have to work feeling like a pincushion, Gibson had to overcome his fear of flying. He hates flying. He looks at aircraft with the same suspicion a desert dweller might have for a canoe, which for *Air*

America was a problem since the actors spent almost as much time in the air as on terra firma.

There was only one way Gibson could face those fears. He would have to learn to fly the bastards.

He didn't actually get a certificate to pilot a Boeing 747, but he did learn to take a helicopter up and down. 'When I started my instructor told me putting a helicopter down was like landing on a greased golf ball. Well, it wasn't just like landing on a greased golf ball. It was like trying to hump in a hamaock. Very, very tricky.'

As filming progessed events became increasingly bizarre. Some crew members were grumbling that it would have been easier making the movie where there weren't so many goddamned Asians. The problem was the movie was about Southeast Asia and wouldn't have been the same with, say, Mexicans. What was getting up their noses was the Thai way of nodding the head and saying, no problem, when in fact there was every problem in the world. And the rain had been getting on their nerves. In a Hollywood back lot the rain can be controlled. Here it had been coming down so hard the crew wouldn't have been surprised to see Noah come of the jungle followed by a variety of animals. Director Spottiswoode, who wanted clear weather for a certain sequence, asked the village soothsayer when the rain would stop.

'One hour,' said the soothsayer, with the confidence of a television weatherman.

Though the rain kept falling like the sky had developed a permanent leak, sixty minutes later it stopped as suddenly as it had begun. As the soothsayer turned and walked away, he muttered: 'Earthquake come now.'

Sure enough, two days later, at the inconvenient hour of 4am, the earth rumbled, sending some of Hollywood's biggest names into the corridors, not all wearing their silk pyjamas from Rodeo Drive. (There were no reports of anyone emerging from a room not registered in their name.) Some were pale of face, either because they had seen too many movies about earthquakes or because they had forgotten to take their Lomotil. A few old Hollywood hands sauntered out. They had been through tremors before, not all originating in the San Andreas fault.

The earthquake was a sizeable one, 6.1 on the Richter scale, causing Gibson to describe it in terms more colourful than accurate: 'You wake up at four in the morning and see the chandelier swinging up and snapping on the ceiling and you see the top of the building touch the pavement. At 6.1 it was a big jolt, just short of the building falling over. I stood in a doorway and things were really jumping. But you can't beat the rush of adrenalin. Whoosh! With an earthquake you really know you're ALIVE.'

What impressed people working on the film was the way Gibson regarded himself as 'just one of the boys', whether it was skylarking with technicians or cooking on a barbecue for the crew. One of the highest paid stars in the world, he could have demanded this and that, complained to his agent if it wasn't available, thrown tantrums, indulged in a little temperament. This is the way of many stars. 'The only thing Mel demands is that he's treated like everyone else,' Daniel Melnick said. 'He doesn't want star treatment. He eats in the hot sun during lunch breaks with everybody else and he's most comfortable standing around talking with the cast and crew.'

Only once did Gibson blow his stack during *Air America*. He regretted it immediately. 'I got pissed off, yelled at somebody and felt terrible. Everyone goes quiet. You've broken the thread. It's not worth it.'

Gibson and company spent three months in Thailand. His sixth child was born while he was running around the jungles.

When the film was released it was not greeted with as much enthusiasm as the producers had hoped, indeed had banked their money on. Maybe the reason was *Air America* was more a comedy than a drama and a lot of people thought there was nothing especially funny about the weird activities of the clandestine airline. They couldn't get many laughs out of the CIA helping run one hundred per cent pure heroin. They couldn't, the kids who shot up the stuff couldn't and cops facing drug dealers toting automatic weapons couldn't. There's not a load of laughs in smack.

Reporter Robert Sam Anson, who covered the war in Laos and drank with the real Air America pilots at the real White Rose bar, not an ambassador in sight, summed up his attitude with these words: 'All we've left out is why the CIA went into the opium-hauling business and how, because of it, a lot of real, innocent people died.

'You'll just have to see the movie.

'Not that it'll tell you, either.'

No one was angrier at what appeared on screen than British journalist

Christopher Robbins, on whose book, *Air America*, the film had been based. The book was published in 1979 after Robbins had spent considerable time investigating the airline, its connection with the CIA, what it carried and why.

He was appalled at Hollywood's interpretation. 'The film is a very trivial comedy about a tragedy – 100,000 people were killed,' he said. 'The one thing had you asked me not to do with the book would be to make it into a comedy . . . I just couldn't believe it. I thought that at least it would have been interesting. But it went the way of many things in Hollywood. They put thirty-five million dollars in one end and a turkey came out the other end.'

Maybe Robbins should have expected nothing better. *Air America* was, after all, made by the film company, Carolco. The same company was responsible for *Rambo*.

13

Gibson, Prince of Hamlets

Mel Gibson had not long been in England preparing for his role in *Hamlet* when he picked up the telephone and dialled the United States home of actress Glenn Close, who had been signed to play Hamlet's mother, Queen Gertrude. He was in a talkative mood. He had a lot of things on his mind. One of the things on his mind was the way people had reacted to the news he was to play the melancholy prince of Denmark.

Some thought it a huge joke. They reckoned *Hamlet* should be retitled *Omelette* because Gibson would have egg all over his face. Or maybe it should be called *Lethal Bodkin*. Others suggested the next move would be to sign Sylvester Stallone for Romeo. And, Jesus, the accent. He'd turn a soliloquy into a call for the cows to come home. A number thought of the great Hamlets, portrayed by such as Laurence Olivier, John Gielgud, Alec Guinness, Derek Jacobi, Nicol Williamson and shuddered because here was an actor known for his characterization of Mad Max and Martin Riggs with the hide to tackle one of the most difficult and great roles in the English language. To play Hamlet, an actor was supposed to have studied at the Royal Academy of Dramatic Art or the Central School of Speech Training and Dramatic Art, starved with little repertory companies in the north of England, worked for peanuts at the Shakespeare Memorial Theatre in Statford-upon-Avon, auditioned for Joan Littlewood . . . to have paid his dues (and his British Actors' Equity fees) before he could put Hamlet on the big screen – not just make pictures people actually wanted to see.

A tabloid newspaper guffawed: 'Mad Max To Play Crazy Dane'.

But Gibson wasn't worried. He was quite relaxed when he telephoned

Glenn Close. 'Everyone's laughing at me over here,' he said. 'But screw 'em.'

Gibson had fewer doubts than his critics because he knew what his critics had forgotten, that his background was in classical theatre. Shakespeare had been high on the agenda when he studied at the National Institute of Dramatic Art in Sydney. He had played Romeo. He was even considered for Hamlet, but rejected on the grounds he was too young.

The Italian director Franco Zeffirelli, an eccentric and sometimes difficult man, had long wanted to film *Hamlet*. He knew what he was about when it came to putting the Bard on the screen. In the Sixties he had made a sexy *Romeo and Juliet*, which had grossed around $A130 million (£60 million) and teamed Richard Burton and Elizabeth Taylor in *The Taming of The Shrew*. But *Hamlet* had always eluded him on film, although he had directed it on the stage in 1964. He tried unsuccessfully to do another stage production in Los Angeles in 1979 with Richard Gere in the title role.

He knew what he wanted. 'I must break with tradition,' he said before the cameras had rolled. 'I never loved this self-masturbating, blond, impotent, supposedly romantic prince who is presented as the definitive Hamlet. Hell, the role has been so emasculated, it has been played by women. He is fit enough to fight a duel and I think he is the opposite of vulnerable. He knows about the dealings of the world but he had a divided heart. He sees his duty but can't bring himself to do it.'

Zeffirelli had long admired Gibson's work, going back to *Gallipoli*. He had watched fascinated as Gibson strode through the *Mad Max* movies which hardly had any lines of dialogue at all and was moved by his performance in *Lethal Weapon*.

'He has stature,' Zeffirelli enthused. 'I was impressed by him. I began to think here is my Hamlet . . . It was the voice. I was madly in love with the voice.'

On being approached for the role, over a plate of spaghetti in the Four Seasons Hotel in Los Angeles, Gibson was uncertain. He kept thinking, hell, why do a play that's been around four hundred years, that's been done to death, that's going to make you the target of every critic from Argentina to Zambia. After reading the play for Zeffirelli, he changed his mind.

Once he had agreed, Zeffirelli could breathe more easily. Gibson was the key to making the film. With his name on the dotted line there would be no shortage of finance, even from Hollywood moguls who were thinking maybe Gibson had gone nuts. In fact Gibson's own company, Icon, put up a large part of the budget.

'He put his life and career there,' said Zeffirelli in admiration. 'Imagine if he did not succeed. He would have been the joke of the industry.'

Other actors were signed, each intrigued by the prospect of being involved with such an unexpected choice as Gibson. Glenn Close said her initial reaction was: 'Why not? I've always loved his work, particularly when I saw him in *Lethal Weapon* in that scene where he was contemplating suicide. I thought he had the imagination of an actor who has resources which are yet to be challenged.'

Helena Bonham-Carter, signed for Ophelia, said she was 'sort of surprised. Everyone was surprised. But then I thought it could have been a genius move. First of all, I realized Mel was not going to be a fool and if he couldn't give a good shot at the part he wouldn't do it.'

While many around him were wondering and worrying about the project, Gibson got himself into training. Probably the hardest part was to stop smoking and give his throat and lungs a chance to cope with the long passages of Elizabethan language. Instead of his one or two packets of Marlboro a day, he exercised his jaws with nicotine chewing gum, removing the wad only when launching into his lines. Being more expert with a gun than a sword, he was taught the ballet-like intricacies of fencing; Hamlet was a master swordsman. That he had to learn to ride a horse may seem odd for a man who runs cattle properties. But then in this unromantic, more practical age horses on cattle properties are like nipples on men – decorative, perhaps, but not especially useful. Today's cattlemen ride motorbikes.

And all the time the thought of playing Hamlet niggled away at the back of his mind. Not so much that he was playing the part, but how he would play it. 'I couldn't sleep at night with this character,' he said. 'It was like something that kind of ruled your whole life . . .'

He was later to say: 'There are moments playing Hamlet that make you want to rip your hair out because he is the most confounding character ever written. The only consistent thing about Hamlet is his inconsistency, and you're chasing your tail. You feel like you're going mad – and you do, a little bit . . .'

For the shoot at Shepperton Studios and locations in castles along the Kent and Scottish coasts, Gibson moved his family into an eight-bedroom house with an acre of land. Sometimes his wife Robyn would visit the set with their six-year-old twins, Edward and Christian, to watch some of the film. Gibson felt secure with his wife and family close, knowing he could get away from the complexities of his character to the relative peace of home – if a home with six kids can be peaceful. He flew his parents, Hutton and Anne Gibson, from Australia to watch proceedings.

Dunnottar Castle in Scotland became Elsinore. But filming there didn't go according to the script. Shakespeare emphasized the gloom of Elsinore but when the crew got there it was as sunny as an advertisement for Butlin's. Much time and expense was spent blocking out the sun.

The role was physically demanding. Gibson had to be sewn into his costume which caused him to sweat profusely beneath the hot lights. A back problem didn't help. At one stage, filming was delayed for twenty-four hours after he strained his back lifting an actor.

Enjoying his pranks and puns, which were not getting any better, the other actors began to look at him with new respect. Alan Bates, who played Claudius, said simply: 'Mel Gibson is brilliant. He is going to surprise a lot of people.'

Ian Holm (Polonius) said he had nothing but admiration for Gibson. 'It's a hell of a thing for a megastar of his magnitude to put himself on the line by playing Hamlet with a lot of Brits. He does just fine.'

Helena Bonham-Carter, who spent considerable time being thrown around by Gibson, enjoyed some of his humour. 'He's a real clown, a buffoon. He is so relaxed when you're actually with him,' she said.

Production was completed after five months and Gibson waited for the slings and arrows he suspected would come from the critics. In recent years he had not worried about critics, perhaps agreeing with the comment of Brendan Behan: 'Critics are like eunuchs in a harem – they know how it's done, they see it done every day but they're unable to do it themselves.'

At the same time Gibson was savvy enough to know that a film like *Hamlet* could be destroyed by the critics. The people who read film criticism in newspapers and magazines were the same people who were *Hamlet*'s potential audience. With films like *Lethal Weapon* it didn't matter much what the critics had to say, but *Hamlet* . . . well, all he could do

Gibson got some seriously good reviews for his playing of the title role in *Hamlet*.

when making it was follow Shakespeare's advice, also from *Hamlet*: 'Speak the speech, I pray you, as I pronounced it to you, trippingly on the tongue; but if you mouth it, as many of your players do, I had as lief the town-crier spoke my lines. Nor do not saw the air too much with your hand, but use all gently; for in the very torrent, tempest, and – as I may say – whirlwind of passion, you must acquire and beget a temperance, that may give it smoothness.'

Before it was shown publicly, he confessed: 'It's the hardest damn thing I've ever tried to do. It's beaten a lot of guys and it might have beaten me. I don't know. The way they did it, when they slice it up, it mightn't work. I don't have an idea. After this everything is going to be a cakewalk.'

Leaving nothing to chance, Gibson embarked on an arduous world-wide publicity tour. He didn't have to worry about empty chairs at press conferences. Every show business reporter wanted to have a few words with Gibson, though not necessarily about *Hamlet*. Gibson didn't mind, he got his plug in, anyway.

Part of his pre-release preparations was to make an educational video on *Hamlet*, which he did in co-operation with students of University High in Los Angeles. He talked to them about Hamlet in their own language . . . 'great story . . . eight violent deaths, murder, incest, adultery, a mad woman, poison, revenge . . . and sword fights'.

The students, who had thought Shakespeare about as much fun as a George Bush speech, were delighted. 'I asked them a lot of questions,' said Gibson. 'They couldn't answer them but it got them thinking about the play. Some of these questions I couldn't answer myself because Shakespeare doesn't come to any answers. He was just raising the questions; that is what is so intriguing.'

Then, on the eve of what was to be his greatest triumph, tragedy came into his life. It was December 1990. His mother, who had been ill for some time with diabetes and a heart condition, died at the age of sixty-nine. Gibson was shattered. Catching the first available plane, he arrived in Australia weary and pale after a twenty-hour flight from Los Angeles.

In the Kiewa Valley his friends and neighbours and people who knew him only by name placed a protective screen around him. As a local police-man said: 'It's not going to be a publicity occasion, I'll tell you that.'

A shopkeeper, who asked not to be named, said the community would not let the family suffer any more than it had. 'They're part and parcel of our community. Fitted in like gloves from the very first day. Mel's just one of us when he's home on the farm.'

Across in America a longtime Gibson family friend, Ed Stinson, was grief-stricken. 'I wondered what his Mum would have thought of his Hamlet,' he said. 'When Mel flew Anne and Hutton to England for a visit to the *Hamlet* location, Anne called me and invited Virginia [his wife] and myself to fly over to London for a reunion. But Virginia wasn't well and the timing was off. Then Anne passed away. I tried three times to write a letter to Hutton and family, but it was too difficult . . . I choked on all three. They're special people, the Gibsons . . . But thank heavens for the memories . . . you can't take them away.'

Saddened that his mother never had the opportunity to see him in *Hamlet*, Gibson flew back to Los Angeles to continue the publicity rounds. Paul Dougherty, an Australian reporter based in Hollywood, expressed surprise to a Warner Bros executive that Gibson could face the press so soon after the funeral.

'We're as surprised as you are that he came back to do this, but of course we're delighted,' the executive told Dougherty. 'It's an indication of how important he feels this film is that he would lay himself on the line for the press and all the public appearances, at a time when this must be the last place he would want to be.'

The executive warned Dougherty, as he did other reporters, not to mention Anne Hutton's death, or even offer condolences. Dougherty noticed that Gibson, who was dressed sombrely in a black suit over a black and beige polo shirt, was smoking again. There was tension in the room. Dougherty felt tense himself as he asked Gibson what it was like to have Glenn Close, who at forty-three was not that much older than Gibson, playing his mother.

'It was fantastic,' he said. 'She was so good I think I'll adopt her.'

The atmosphere suddenly electrified. Gibson's voice dropped to a mumble. 'She's great to work with . . . but young to be my mother . . .' A silence filled the room as his voice trailed off.

Dougherty realized then that the mention of Glenn Close playing his mother had triggered off an awareness that he no longer had a mother of his own. 'It's a thing that keeps happening to people in the first few weeks after a parent dies before they have really come to accept it,' reasoned Dougherty.

Gibson was now waiting anxiously for the American reviews. He understood the critics were poised with sharpened pencils and would insert them deeply into his career. Some would rather bury him than praise him. But by the end of December he knew he had pulled it off.

Said the *New York Times*: 'Mel Gibson's Hamlet is strong, intelligent and safely beyond ridicule. He is a visceral Hamlet, tortured by his own thoughts and passions, confused by his recognition of evil, a Hamlet whose emotions are raw yet who retains the desperate wit to act mad. He is by far the best part of Mr Zeffirelli's sometimes slick but always lucid and beautifully cinematic version of the play.'

Praise indeed from America's most respected newspaper. More was to come. *USA Today* said: 'It's a triumph few could've predicted . . .'

New York Post: 'Yes, Mel Gibson makes a very good Hamlet. By my troth, a *very* good Hamlet, and it's a doubly pleasant surprise, since all we've had to judge him by are the likes of *Mad Max* and *Lethal Weapon*, in which dilemmas are more easily resolved with fisticuffs than with soliloquy . . .'

New York News: 'Those who come to mock this strutting Hollywood player may be surprised by his vigorous self-assured performance.'

Toronto Globe and Mail: 'Okay, let's get the obvious question out of the way first. Mel Gibson cast as Hamlet? You bet, and he's just fine, thank you. Not stellar or definitive, but entirely of a piece with what is a defiantly cinematic reading of the play . . .'

With reviews like those, Gibson knew his acting gamble had not only worked but that *Hamlet* was likely to do well at the box office. He may have recalled the quip from his *Air America* co-star, Robert Downey Jr: 'Either Mel will get an Academy Award or it will be the first time Shakespeare ever grossed a hundred million dollars.'

Confident and relaxed, Gibson returned to Australia to something of a hero's welcome, especially when he visited his old alma mater, the National Institute of Dramatic Art. One reason for returning to NIDA was to announce the Mel Gibson–Village Roadshow–NIDA scholarship for a student on either technical or creative courses.

Another reason was to talk to students. The school theatre was packed

Mel Gibson and his wife Robyn attend the 1989 Oscars at Los Angeles.

for his appearance, the students hanging on every word, cheering every statement. He was what they all aspired to be – an actor with box office appeal who could tackle the classics successfully.

He was asked if he would be haunted forever by the role of the tormented Hamlet. 'I'm not going to let the bugger bother me,' he joked, dropping the line like a professional comic.

Asked about the way the tabloid newspapers had greeted the announcement he would play Hamlet, he replied: 'Who cares? I don't. I'm rich.'

This is what the students wanted to hear, for inside every actor there is not a singer struggling to get out, or even a comic, but a millionaire. In his cream suit, Gibson was the realization of their own dreams.

Before the Australian première of *Hamlet*, held in Sydney, Gibson mingled at a party with invited guests, a cigarette in his mouth, a beer in his hand, always with women gazing at him like they wished to take him home right then.

He tried to explain to a reporter why *Hamlet* was important to him. 'I want this production to be successful because I love Shakespeare and the world needs more Shakespeare ... because it's full of wisdom, wit and beauty. We need more of that and less of ... like a weekend trip to a knocking shop.'

After the party, guests moved to the cinema. It says a lot for Gibson's character and style that he did not roll up in a limousine playing the star, waving to people he didn't know and shaking hands with people he may have detested. Instead, he slipped quietly up the stairs and, ignoring the rows of seats reserved exclusively for VIPs, took an unreserved seat at the side. When the lights went up on an applauding audience, Gibson had already vanished.

The Australian press was as enthusiastic about *Hamlet* as had been the American press. Evan Williams, in *The Australian*, commented: 'Having seen *Hamlet* I feel I should take back all the unkind things I've said about Mel Gibson over the years. He's done something brave and important ...'

The *Sunday Telegraph* thought Shakespeare would not be turning in his grave over the Gibson interpretation. 'I rather think he would be proud to see one of his best works so well handled,' wrote Paul LePetit.

Bev Tivey, in the *Sydney Telegraph Mirror*, said Gibson gave an admirable performance, 'a perfect balance of thinker and man of action. He

Mel Gibson had to learn to ride a horse for this scene in *Hamlet*.

presents a vigorous, resolute Hamlet, not a vacillating wimp, but a man who knows exactly what he must do, but hates having to do it.'

Gibson had one more field to conquer, Britain, the toughest of all. Serious British critics had looked with suspicion at the entire venture, unable to see much beyond Gibson's characters of Mad Max and Martin Riggs. They also considered themselves the keepers of the flame. Only they knew and understood the traditions and grandeur of Shakespeare. What would a Hollywood matinée idol know. Especially one who had spent most of his life in, for God's sake, Australia, where philistines are heroes and intellectuals considered queer.

After the British première – a royal affair attended by the intellectual Duchess of York – came the reviews. The critics thought him better than expected but still felt compelled to sneer.

The *Guardian* said: 'He makes a plain-spoken rather uncomplicated Hamlet who sometimes seems scarcely to know what's hitting him but bravely tries to mould fate to his own ends all the same.'

The Times accused Gibson of enunciating 'with the unreal clarity of a speaking clock'. The newspaper went on: 'He is grave, anguished, tender, playful, all the things Hamlet should be. Yet, though Mel Gibson is never for one moment bad, almost everybody else in the cast is better. And for all his efforts we never get under this Hamlet's skin. Mel Gibson's Hamlet appears decent, slick, easily digestible: a fast-food Hamlet for the moment, without the stature to make it a Hamlet for the ages.'

After doing everything possible to promote *Hamlet*, Gibson went back to his farm. He badly needed a rest after making three movies – *Bird on a Wire*, *Air America* and *Hamlet* – back to back. The last time he did three movies back to back it almost destroyed him. 'You work because you want to work and you're hungry,' he told Hollywood reporter Jenny Cooney. 'Then you wait till you're full and you take a break. You have to take a break, to do the things that you work for, or you couldn't survive.'

Even resting, he had his eye on several projects. One movie, *The Rest of Daniel*, a fantasy comedy about a man frozen for fifty years in a cryogenics experiment, has the most expensive script in Hollywood history, its writer, Jeffrey Abrams, getting $A2.45 (over £1 million). He also looked at a western and a film based on American correspondent, George Polk, who was found in a Greek harbour shot through the back of the neck, probably on the orders of the CIA and the then right-wing Greek government. *Lethal Weapon III* will also go before the cameras. After considering the options Gibson selected the Polk story, and signed controversial Greek director Costa-Gavras, who has won two Academy Awards for his no-punches-pulled political films *Z*, about the Greek Fascist Colonels, and *Missing*, set in El Salvador.

He is not worried about money. After hearing Gibson would play Hamlet, the director of *Air America*, Roger Spottiswoode, observed: 'After *Hamlet*, Mel's asking price will be ten or eleven million dollars.'

Spottiswoode wasn't far out. In February 1991, Gibson's lawyers in Los Angeles finalized an astounding $A100 million (£46 million) four-picture deal which will make him one of the most powerful actors in cinema history. His fee will rise to $A10 million (£4.5 million) and finally, $A15 million (£6.8 million) during the span of the new contract with Warner Bros. 'Money is not a problem – getting Mel Gibson is,' a Warner spokesman was reported as saying.

The deal was signed with Gibson's own company, Icon Productions, which will pay Gibson as an actor and executive producer or producer. Icon will pay for scripts.

It's a far cry from 1976 when he was paid $A400 for his first movie, *Summer City*. Since then his fees have been: *Mad Max* (1977) $A15,000, *Tim* (1978) $A30,000, *Attack Force Z* (1978) $A35,000, *Gallipoli* (1980) $A50,000, *Mad Max II* (1981) $A120,000, *The Year of Living Dangerously* (1982) $A250,000, *The Bounty* (1983) $A400,000, *The River* (1984) $A500,000, *Mrs Soffel* (1984) $A700,000, *Mad Max Beyond Thunderdome* (1985) $A1,200,000, *Lethal Weapon* (1987) $A1,500,000, *Tequila Sunrise* (1988) $A2,000,000, *Lethal Weapon II* (1988) $A3,000,000, *Bird on a Wire* (1990) $A4,400,000, *Air America* (1990) $A5,600,000. For *Hamlet* (1990) he took a huge salary cut down to $A1,000,000, but had a percentage deal and was a major investor.

That Gibson is the most bankable movie star in the world is not disputed. His name on a picture contract ensures financial backing; his name on the cinema marquee almost guarantees it will be a box office success. 'They'd give you money for Mel's film even if he was starring in a screen version of the telephone directory,' said one astute Los Angeles casting director.

In May 1990, the prestigious *Premiere* magazine listed the one hundred most powerful people in Hollywood. Gibson was number 46. The only actors ahead of him were Tom Cruise (15), Eddie Murphy (17), Arnold Schwarzenegger (20), Sylvester Stallone (34), Jack Nicholson (36), Robert Redford (45), Danny De Vito (43), Michael Douglas (44) and Warren Beatty (45). The magazine pointed out the importance of power in Hollywood: 'When it comes to the movie business, power means more than green-lighting projects or grossing big at the box office. What distinguishes the powerful is the influence they wield over others – through respect, admiration or fear. Power is Hollywood's most sought-after quality . . .'

By the beginning of 1991, with *Hamlet* both a critical and financial success, a new list would have Gibson among the leaders. And he's likely to stay there for as long as he wishes, outlasting Arnie and Sly who soon will be too old to flex their muscles in public.

Financially he need never work again. He knows the fickleness of fans and understands that one day they will not queue at the box office just because his name is on the posters.

'People must be sick of me, or they will be soon,' he said.

When that day comes he will return to his farm in the Kiewa Valley, not only to raise cattle but to find the anonymity and privacy he craves.